THE APPIAN WAY

The people, the places and the history of the road that led to Europe

DAVID HEWSON

CONTENTS

Introduction   v

PART I
THE WOLF WAKES

1. Modest Beginnings   3
2. Enter the Censor   12
3. The Road to War   18
4. Enter the Greeks   29

PART II
THEY MAKE A DESERT AND CALL IT PEACE

5. The End of the Road is the Beginning   45
6. Hannibal at the Gates   50
7. A Dictator in the Wings   66
8. The Slaves Strike Back   77
9. Life Beyond the Wars   91

PART III
THE AGE OF EMPERORS

10. Octavian Grows up... quickly   101
11. The View from the Coast   103
12. An Emperor in the Making   115
13. A Poet with a Mission   123
14. Even Gods Die   133

PART IV
DECLINE AND FALL

15. The Priest in the Hills   141
16. The Rich Grow Ever Richer   150
17. Back to the Eternal City   155
18. The Road of the Dead   159
19. One God and One Alone   167
20. Rome's Last Days   180

INFORMATION FOR TRAVELLERS

Take your time   193

About the Author   203

INTRODUCTION

The problem with history is people think it's all about the past. Long ago when I was at school the subject seemed done and very much dusted. Everything that went before was distant, fixed, defined, as solid and unchanging as the walls of the Tower of London, the people who populated those bygone years as stiff and dead as the calcified victims of Pompeii.

It was as if those far-off times were inhabited by a different species altogether. They were primitives, especially beyond the English Channel. Relatives of ours, it's true, but ones you felt you ought to acknowledge while hoping they'd never turn up for tea. After all, this was the second half of the twentieth century. A brave new world beckoned, one of jet travel and motorways, television and the birth of electronics. The white heat of technology, Harold Wilson, our Prime Minister, called it. A world the ancients could never begin to understand. We were modern people, civilised, settled, scientific, rational, far removed from the natives of previous generations grubbing around in the muck and blood of their squalid lives. The onward march of Darwinism was relentless as we left the primordial chaos of yesterday to evolve into... what?

That wasn't a question you were supposed to ask. History was all about the dead and buried. The future was ours alone to invent. Why question an opportunity like that? All you had to do was wait and watch our world get better and better.

Even as an eleven-year-old, living in a council flat on the chilly coast of Yorkshire, no money in the family, no chance I might ever see another country soon, perhaps ever, question it I did. The more I looked beyond the ancient, blinkered textbooks school gave me, the more the picture they offered seemed distinctly fuzzy and wrong. We did have a black and white telly and I could see the news was full of dire warnings about the Cold War and nuclear Armageddon. Just before I went to 'big school' the President of the United States was assassinated in public, much like so many Roman emperors of old. The principal difference was that we knew about his savage murder in hours and could watch the bloody tragedy unfold in grainy black and white right there in front of us at home.

Our world was faster and more slickly connected than ever. But were we really different? Not if the books I kept borrowing from the public library were to be believed. While the school teachers harped on about ziggurats and hieroglyphics, rarely individuals – people – at all, my head was somewhere else altogether. First came the stories of Mary Renault who brought ancient Macedon and Alexander the Great to life. Then Robert Graves followed and I found myself in the poisonous and all-too-real court of imperial Rome as the crippled Claudius struggled to survive among his murderous, scheming relatives.

This didn't seem like 'history' at all. It felt like real life. And yes, Renault and Graves were novelists who took liberties with their source material to tell a cracking tale. All the same, in between Latin lessons, I could go back to that same library and the books they read, the histories of Tacitus and Livy, Sallust and Cassius Dio, the endless letters of the voluble Cicero who had an opinion on everything under the sun, and one day would pay for it dearly as we'll come to hear.

A picture of Italy began to form in my teenage mind. A bright world full of colour and drama, peopled by larger-than-life characters, warmed by constant sun, rich with wine and exotic food. A place very unlike the cold, bleak coast of Yorkshire.

The more I read, something else began to form in my imagination too. It was a road, long and straight, a vital artery the Romans created. One that seemed to link everything and everyone across the centuries, tying together their stories into a web of ambition, tragedy, heroism and, above all, a burgeoning sense of civilisation.

There were drawings of this road, a narrow cobbled pavement just wide enough to take two carts side-by-side. Near the cities tombs rose by the wayside, some like small columned temples, others more tiny castles, fortresses in marble. Out in the countryside tall cypress trees took their place, standing like exclamation marks, along with avenues of stately stone pines, their leafy umbrellas shielding the highway as it stretched off into the distance.

It was called the Via Appia, the Appian Way, 'Regina Viarum', the Queen of Roads. One day, I promised myself, I'd take a journey along that road. Perhaps walk, ride a horse or take a scooter all the way from Rome down to the southern shore of the Adriatic Sea where it ended.

I didn't linger in Yorkshire. Soon opportunity and ambition took me to London and a job in newspapers. Before long I was travelling the Europe I'd read about. After a while making the trek as a novelist too, a storyteller weaving fables in Rome and Venice, Amsterdam and Copenhagen, moving about as freely as I wanted, by plane, by train or car. The Via Appia was a teenage dream. We all have them. One I always remembered whenever I came back to Claudius, the fearful, stammering emperor of Robert Graves or picked up Livy or Tacitus again. But a tick on a wish list I never thought I'd get round to.

Then, one strange morning in 2016, I woke up to discover the country I thought I'd been living in – as contented as modern societies got, connected, fluid, mobile – seemed to be a myth. Instead of talking about roads and the right to move freely from nation to nation, the news concerned barriers and borders, and how my fellow Europeans were foreigners we didn't really want or need. Before long this strange and, to me, alien mood spread across the Atlantic and the talk turned to building walls. Keeping people out instead of letting them in.

Rome has left us with so many legacies. Language and laws, architecture, religion, political structures and even a couple of months of the year named after men who died two millennia ago, one murdered by his peers, the other doing the murdering to seize the imperial crown. From what I recalled the pioneering Romans of old didn't get there by cowering behind their walls.

So half a century after I first made that vow I finally set off on a journey to discover the Via Appia... and try to work out if I'd read it wrong all these years.

I had, though not in any way I'd expected. What I found wasn't the picturesque, idyllic highway of my imagination, stretching out past ruined temples into a pastoral countryside of cypress trees and stone pines. That's mostly gone. In its place I came across something more subtle and more interesting, a tale of people and places, of trade and commerce and politics that's as pertinent now as it was when Caesar stalked the Forum and Cicero penned his bitchy letters to his friends. Those three hundred and fifty miles of cobblestones helped turn a minor Italian state into the masters of an empire that stretched from Britain to Babylon, from the Atlantic coastline of North Africa to the shores of the Black Sea.

The Italian word for 'history' is *storia*. And so's the Italian for 'story' too. So this is a little of both, a journey like all stories truly are, a narrative of unintended consequences that shows we're here today, shaped by the Romans and their love of building roads, as much by accident as planning. A story, I hope, that tells us history isn't about the past so much as where we came from. And where we may be headed too.

It's a tale more full of myths and shadows and mysteries than I ever expected when I finally set out on my much-delayed adventure one sunny September afternoon. Even the place we start isn't where you might think.

Follow my journey online with photos and an interactive Google Earth map at www.davidhewson.com/appian.

THE WOLF WAKES

The Via Appia running through Minturnae

❧ I ❦

MODEST BEGINNINGS

I MEET my road trip companion at Fiumicino airport. As a nod to Italy it's an Abarth 595, basically a cute Fiat 500 variation with the engine of a racing car under the bonnet. The two of us are about to cover fourteen hundred miles driving to Brindisi and back. One thing I discover very quickly as I steer my pocket rocket into Rome: if you're in a lane on your own as you try to navigate the inexplicable traffic system around Piramide that's probably because you're going the wrong way down a tram track. Another revelation came soon after: you can read all the books you like back home but Italy in the raw will turn your head around and teach you something different.

When I started out, full of research and itineraries, I had it in mind that this would be the story of a trip along the old road, north to south. A few days in I find myself walking down a grubby lane past a sign that reads 'Via Appia Antica', rapidly beginning to realise it's all more complicated than that. This is a story to be told more from a chronological point of view than a geographical one. A tale of culture, history and politics, not places along the way.

Where I find myself is a million miles from the tourist view of classical Italy. There's fly tipping everywhere, bags of rubbish, a rusting washing machine, what looks like discarded food rotting in the weeds along the verge. Graffiti shrieks about fascists in the police while a mountain of old tyres leans over the crumbling wall to one side. Around the corner sits a grimy coach park for the station where local trains stand by a siding, seemingly at the end of the old road, waiting for someone to board. It feels like the back of beyond. No, it *is* the back of beyond. But this is a stretch of the Via Appia Antica or what's left of it, and I'm looking for something important.

Finally, after asking the one puzzled local I manage to find, who clearly thinks I'm a little mad, I reach it. Past an unremarkable white church and yet more parked-up buses, sits a four-arch, humpback bridge which, not so long ago, allowed cars across its shiny, carefully laid patterned cobblestones. They're banned now so hardly anyone finds their way here. I sit on the wall for a while, watch the languid river flow past beneath me and try to imagine another time, two thousand three hundred years before, when the construction of this little bridge marked the death of one civilisation and the rise to mighty power of another.

It's now called the Ponte Leproso after a leper hospital that once stood nearby, but back then it was the point at which the Via Appia entered Benevento. This was Beneventum to the Romans, thirty miles north east of Naples, set on a hill above the rivers Calore and Sabato. Twenty minutes on foot from the scruffy area around the station where the Ponte Leproso sits, I find a prosperous-looking town with an elegant, student-filled centre and plenty of fertile countryside around producing good local wine and olive oil. Few tourists make their way here, and those that do are often in search of its legendary witches, supposedly priestesses of Isis who could fly with a little help from some magic ointment while congregating around a mystical walnut tree on the banks of the Sabato.

They still come out once a year in September when plenty of the local liqueur Strega – it means 'witch' – goes down the hatch during the annual 'night of the witches', a busy local festival. But there are more traditional sights too since Benevento has been at the centre of Italian history for more than two millennia. Just off the main street I come across a chap walking a handsome donkey into town for reasons I can't imagine, not that any of the locals take much note. Behind him lies the magnificent triumphal Arch of Trajan, depicting the usual victories over barbarians, this time the Dacians who lived by the Danube as it led into the Black Sea. Erected in the first century AD, it's big, it's grand, it's decidedly imperial as Trajan intended, something that wouldn't be out of place in the forum in Rome. A short stroll away sits Santa Sofia, a circular church from 760 AD and the arrival of the invading Lombards. Around the corner is the city museum crammed full of exhibits going back to prehistoric times and down the hill, not far from the Ponte Leproso, sits the inevitable amphitheatre of the kind no Roman city of any size could do without.

Ambling among the sights along the relaxed, pleasant centre street of Corso Garibaldi it's easy to miss a small plaque on the old tower in front of Santa Sofia, one that depicts the balance of power in Italy between the sixth and fourth centuries BC. Beneventum appears as one of the principal cities of 'Il Sannio' – the ancient region of Samnium, home to a family of tribes known collectively as the Samnites. Lucania lies to the south and Apulia to the east. North there's Umbria with Picenum alongside while Latium occupies the western shore of the Tyrrhenian sea.

This simple plaque throws me. I always understood Rome was one city state among many in Italy around then. But Rome is Rome, and we tend to assume it was great and powerful and ambitious from the start. That Rome is Italy and Italy Rome. Nothing could be further from the truth. This map shows how much the Samnites dominated the picture, the largest state of all, stretching from below the Amalfi coast through Pompeii past Naples in the west, across the Apennines to the Adriatic, then north to modern day Norcia in Umbria. All its principal cities are there, Neapolis (Naples – I'll give modern names in brackets where appropriate from this point on), Pompeii, Nola along with a few – Corfinium, Amiternum, Cumae – which are now principally ruins and thesis subjects for archaeologists.

Looking at that map, if you wanted to place your bets on which one of those players would come to dominate Italy you might think your money would be safest on the Samnites. Yet today their language is long lost, their culture the stuff of museums and university courses. No one ever asks, 'What did the Samnites do for us?' because, frankly, the answer would be... nothing that we know of.

Instead, that prize would fall to the smallest state of all, squeezed on all sides by more populous neighbours, the Samnites, the Latins, the Umbrians and the Etruscans. Rome, fired by an accidental spark of ignominy that would drive that bridge across the Sabato river in the space of a single generation.

~

TERRITORY WAS something the Samnites had in abundance. Power, people and influence are something else. In the third century BC, Rome may have appeared a minor player on the map but in truth it was turning into one of Italy's more ambitious city states, developing institutions and a kind of political nous missing elsewhere. The place wasn't much to look at, or live in. Even the locals complained. The poet Horace, a couple of centuries later, told a friend how hard it was to write surrounded by constant noise and squalor.

> *A builder in heat hurries along with his mules and porters: the crane whirls aloft at one time a stone, at another a great piece of timber: the dismal funerals block the way with their unwieldy carriages: here runs a mad dog, there rushes a sow begrimed with mire.*

Before this trip I hadn't been in Rome for the best part of a decade. All my Italian friends warned me I was in for a shock. They were right too. Today the wild boars are back foraging the suburbs, feeding on the rubbish left behind by a failed city administration that occasionally seems hellbent on turning back the clock. The traffic's more gridlocked than I remember all around the centre, the city's public transport system a mess. Rome's a place that might seem familiar to someone magically transported into its 21st century guise from the squalor of two millennia ago. Horace, however, is rather given to whining, as we'll hear later in this story – if TripAdvisor was around in his day you imagine he'd scarcely be off it.

Still, the truth remains: the popular image of Rome – gleaming white palaces, temples and arenas – belonged to the later period, when the place lived beneath the thumb of emperors, not the messy, argumentative democratic place it was as a republic. The era of Augustus to be precise, the first of the emperors who was to boast, 'I found Rome a city of bricks and left it a city of marble.'

When this story starts it was a cramped, often squalid community centred around the shallow valley that runs beneath the Palatine. Many of the homes there would be small and primitive in the extreme, the simplest one of the most revered, the Casa Romuli, a mud and straw hut believed to be the home of the city's first king Romulus – you can still see what's thought to be the original site on the Palatine hill. Next to the grandeur of the nearby Forum it's pretty modest to be honest, which is doubtless why few tourists make the long, steep walk to track the spot down amidst all the glorious ruins below. Close by was the Lupercal cave where, the well-known foundation-myth claims, Romulus and his twin brother Remus were raised by a she-wolf. Later the two argued over land and Romulus, or perhaps one of his followers, killed Remus in a fight. After which he founded Rome on April 21st, 753 BC, a date still celebrated by locals as their city's birthday.

Nearly four hundred years after Romulus the city was certainly larger, with a population perhaps approaching 60,000. But unless you came from one of the long-established rich patrician families, the average citizen probably led an impoverished life cooped up in a hovel that hadn't changed much for centuries.

One national characteristic had become apparent over the years, however: when a fight with the neighbours started, and they often did, Rome was pretty much always going to be the last to give in. Tempers had been running high with the Samnites in the south for some time, usually caused by Rome's frequent habit of trying to establish colonies in the territory of others. In 321 BC, after peace talks failed, the Roman army set off to teach their neighbours a lesson.

Disaster was waiting for them and, for a proud race obsessed with honour, something worse: humiliation. Livy takes up the tale from the point of view of the Samnite general, Pontius.

...he sent ten soldiers disguised as shepherds to Calatia (a small town near Capua), where he understood that the Roman consuls were encamped, with instructions to pasture some cattle in different directions near the Roman outposts. When they met any scouting parties, they were all to tell the same story and say that the Samnite legions were in Apulia besieging Lucera with their whole force and that its capture was imminent. This rumour had purposely been spread before and had already reached the ears of the Romans; the captured shepherds confirmed their belief in it, especially as their statements all tallied.

The Romans were fooled into thinking the enemy were miles away, about to take by force a town controlled by their allies. In fact, the wily Pontius had camped his forces much closer, near a pass through the Apennine mountains known as the Caudine Forks. The Romans took the shortest route and walked straight into a trap. Both ends of the defile were controlled by the Samnites who soon blocked every way out, surrounding their enemy so effectively that battle was impossible and surrender the only option.

The encounter was decided without a blow being struck. But this left the Samnites with a dilemma. What did they do with the seven thousand or so hostile soldiers trapped in front of them? While the Romans cowered in the pass, bewailing their ignominious defeat, Pontius's father, Herennius, one of the elder statesmen of the Samnite community, was summoned and asked for an opinion. His advice was simple: negotiate a lasting truce and let the enemy go home. That way they might have a few decades of peace for the first time in years.

The younger Samnites, looking at their trapped enemy's misery, didn't like that idea at all. Fine, said Herennius, in that case kill every last one of them. Put the Romans to the sword on the spot.

Mass executions of captive soldiers were far from rare, though the numbers involved here were rather larger than normal. All the same, the Samnites baulked at the idea of such outright slaughter and came up with a compromise: the Romans would be allowed home, but first they'd have to abandon their weapons and their armour and walk in a plain tunic beneath a makeshift yoke made of spears.

As they left with their tails between their legs Herennius watched, shook his head and uttered a prophetic warning.

This is a policy which wins us no friends and rids us of no enemies. If you let men you've humiliated live, you'll come to regret it. Romans don't know how to remain quiet under defeat. Whatever this disgrace burns into their souls will rankle there forever, and allow them no rest till they've made you pay for it many times over.

Boy, was he right.

~

IF YOU TRAVEL to the Caudine Forks – or where they're supposed to be – you soon start to feel something in this story stinks. The Via Appia runs right through the scene of Rome's shame, now a sleepy part of Campania. It sits on a stretch of the Strada Statale 7 (SS7), a modern road that follows much of Appia's route, between Caserta and Benevento. Two villages, Arpaia and Forchia, maintain a friendly rivalry about which was the actual site of the Samnites' bloodless victory. The only trouble is that, while the mountains certainly narrow in this part of Campania, the terrain doesn't really match the version favoured by Roman historians. It's not a defile in which you can imagine an army being easily trapped.

Perhaps, I thought, trying to work out the geography in my head, there's some exaggeration here. Or the real Caudine Forks were somewhere entirely different. I made a note to remind myself: the stories I'm using to plot my journey and this narrative come down to us from two millennia or more ago. They were often the work of people writing about events that happened a couple of centuries before them. Frequently their version was written with an eye on the politics of the time. Offending someone in power, even inadvertently, was perilous for Roman writers over many centuries. So I repeat: *storia* means both 'history' and 'story', and sometimes it's impossible to discern the line between the two.

That sign in the centre of Benevento whetted my appetite. I wanted to find out more about this mysterious lost tribe, the Samnites, and so I spent a good while wandering the spacious and largely deserted city museum, marvelling at the statues and the relics they'd left behind.

Much of what's survived seems, to the untrained eye, very Roman. While the city in the north and Samnium might have seemed equal opponents in principle, they represented very different societies. The Samnites were no real nation, more a collection of tribes spread across a huge geographical area. For the most part they were nomadic agricultural communities, with few cities to speak of and little in the way of organised leadership. Deeply superstitious, one of their responses to crisis was the 'ver sacrum' or holy spring, a practice in which they promised to dedicate all their children born during a set period of the year to the god Mamers (Mars). Once these unfortunates might have been subject to ritual sacrifice. Later this changed to forced migration; when they became old enough they were expelled from the tribe and told to found their own communities elsewhere. If the tribe was suffering from over-population then perhaps the ritual made some kind of harsh economic sense, but it was hardly a policy for nation-building.

The Samnites had their culture, a sophisticated one as that walk around the Benevento museum demonstrates. They also had their rules. One was compulsory conscription into the army at times of national peril, enforced by capital punishment for any who refused. Nevertheless, there was little in the way of shared purpose, of government and that abiding Roman principle, ambition. Perhaps after the sudden and overwhelming bloodless victory at the Caudine Forks they came to feel they were the big dog in town getting nipped at by a yapping little terrier. In that case it would only be a few years before they realised what they were hearing was the howl of an approaching and relentless wolf.

ROME WAS long past the era of itinerant shepherds and peasant agriculture by the time it squared up to its neighbours in the south. In 509 BC an uprising had ejected the last of its monarchs, Tarquinius, on the grounds of cruelty and tyranny after which the city elders established themselves as guardians of a new republic. The very word 'king' became hated, as Julius Caesar was to discover centuries later. In place of monarchy, Rome came to establish a political structure designed to ensure no one man would ever rule it again. Instead, the city's Senate – men from the upper classes – would elect two 'praetors' to head the government for a single year, each with the power of veto over the other. In time the title was changed to consul, and a series of lower positions came to be created to form an administration that would adapt and evolve to political necessities and changes in the popular mood.

Over decades a system of government came into being that eventually began to resemble a modern state, with elections, factions, delegated responsibilities, checks and balances. Projects were evaluated, budgets set, accounts maintained in an early form of bureaucracy. Above all, there was competition. Romans wanted to succeed, and be seen to do so, whether it was at war, in commerce, or in the midst of the fiery cauldron of politics. Pride and honour came from visible achievement. Public humiliation and disgrace followed failure, sometimes to the point of suicide.

Defeat and surrender were quite foreign, as soon became obvious when the dejected army returned from the Caudine Forks under the terms of a peace treaty that would rapidly turn to ashes. The shame of their surrender would burn into the Roman consciousness until it was expunged the only way they knew, through a final victory. It was coming, too, sooner than the Samnites might ever have expected. Twenty years was all it took for them to lose their last great battle for independence. Before long their language was extinct, their culture swamped by that of their new masters. The Roman wolf was ready to march, hungry to assimilate everyone and everything it met along the way.

All it needed was someone to give it a start.

❧ 2 ❧

ENTER THE CENSOR

IF YOU STAND in the Roman Forum you can spot exactly where the irate senators of 321 BC would have gathered to work how to vent their fury about the debacle in the south. Just find the tall brown, brick building called the Curia Julia. This was the site of the meeting place of the Senate. Imagine instead, somewhere close by, a small temple-like building, at least partly built in wood. No one really knows what the earlier Senate house, the Curia Hostilia, looked like since it was destroyed, burned down when rioters used it to build a pyre for a murdered political thug who'll be making an appearance in this story later.

Today's version is an invention of Mussolini from the 1930s, a reconstruction of the Curia Julia built by Julius Caesar. It never feels authentic to me, though architecturally it's probably pretty close to the original. The ruins of the Forum, the temple bases, the Via Sacra, the flowers on the spot where Caesar was cremated, say more about the past than Mussolini's rather cold and emotionless recreation.

There was a small archaeological dig going on outside the Curia when I was there, which meant the place itself was closed. You see so many of these projects around the Forum that it's easy to forget about them. But a few weeks after my last visit the excavation team made an astonishing announcement: beneath the brown muddy soil in front of the Curia's steps they uncovered a small temple with a circular altar and an empty sarcophagus. This, they now believe, was originally the tomb of Romulus, the legendary founder of Rome.

Somewhere around here in 312 BC a twenty-eight-year-old aristocrat called Appius Claudius Caecus was elected censor. The job had nothing to do with deciding what his fellow citizens could see. The position was that of a powerful senior magistrate with wide powers no other official could easily overturn. Appius was born to power, a scion of the Claudia 'gens', an extended patrician clan that would come to provide Rome with many of its most renowned generals and politicians as well as several emperors. An ambitious and impatient fellow, he was also something of a public speaker. One of his aphorisms the Romans very much liked was the saying 'every man is the architect of his own fortune'. Appius certainly lived up to it.

He didn't wait for his fellow senators in the Curia to approve his ideas. Instead, he immediately raided the state treasury and set in place two large and challenging projects. Since the city was suffering from unreliable water supplies and insanitary conditions, he planned to build an aqueduct, the Aqua Appia, a ten-mile system of pipes that would deliver much-needed clean water directly into the busy commercial quarter known as the Forum Boarium – the stretch of the city by the Tiber where the elegant little circular Temple of Hercules Victor still stands today. This was Rome's first stab at building an aqueduct, and the result turned out to be a ham-fisted, leaky thing that was abandoned a few hundred years later when far better and more sophisticated alternatives were provided by later engineers perfecting Appius's methods.

The road he commissioned was equally adventurous and rather more successful in all respects. Researching my exploration of the Via Appia, I'd come across an extraordinary book published by Princeton University called the *Barrington Atlas of the Greek and Roman World*. This is a massive atlas of the roads of the ancient Greeks and Romans, ranging from the British Isles to the Indian subcontinent and deep into North Africa. The print version costs a whopping £308 but there's an iPad app for a lot less which followed me throughout this trip.

One glance at Map 43, *Latium Vetus*, makes something clear immediately. Highways were nothing new to the Romans of the third and fourth centuries BC. But they were local roads joined to form a connected whole, tracks that existed to link places to the nearest settlement down the way. The better ones would be gravel. Some would be little more than mud tracks. There's nothing to suggest there was anything in the way of organised maintenance. Moving large numbers of troops, wagons and horses around would have been a slow and unpredictable process, at risk of bad weather, poor road surfaces and circuitous journeys.

Appius understood this was no way to fight a war. Rome possessed a formidable military force, but in battle might wasn't everything. The fight against the Samnites meant taking the conflict to their enemy. So speed and manoeuvrability mattered too. Weapons, food, and reinforcements needed to be moved swiftly to the front when they were called for. So his goal was to give the Romans a clear advantage by creating something new: a route specifically for the military that aimed at the contested border.

And there it is in Barrington. A spider's web of roads straggle all the way around Rome, meandering in all directions. Pointing south east is the highway that came to bear Appius's name, heading straight as a die, scarcely a bend in sight until it pops off the page towards the coast and the destination Appius had set, Capua.

Today this is an unassuming place of thirty thousand residents or so with a few historic sites so devoid of visitors they remind you how delightful and different Italy is beyond the tourist treadmill. It's also not the town called that on a map. Some odd name juggling went on during the Middle Ages. The place modern Italy calls Capua was known as Casilinum to the Romans. Their ancient Capua is now Santa Maria Capua Vetere – 'Vetere' being an archaic term for 'ancient' – a few miles away.

Sleepy as it may seem now, for the Romans Capua was a key strategic site, sometimes run by allies, sometimes by leaders they regarded as traitors. An important waypoint on the Via Appia, it will crop up in this story at several critical moments. For Appius, it offered a simple and enticing prospect: if he could drive a reliable, direct new road straight to a friendly outpost at the very edge of Samnite territory the Roman army would be reequipped, fed and reinforced far more quickly and easily than it could along conventional lanes and tracks.

~

THE VIA APPIA began at the Porta Capena gate in the vanished Servian Wall, now a busy road junction next to the Circus Maximus, then ran directly towards the heights of the lush Alban Hills. This stretch near the city is a regional park now, neatly manicured for hordes of modern visitors. I already knew it reasonably well but instinct told me to leave its final exploration to the last when, with a bit of luck, I might understand the context of its tombs and temples and catacombs better.

So I pointed my little Abarth south in Appius's footsteps and headed off into a side of Italy that was, for me, quite unknown. The first narrow cobbled section, running through the Porta San Sebastiano, remains a busy car route, choked with traffic, especially during the rush hour. The cobbles known as Sampietrini don't make for great driving, great walking, and frankly I wouldn't much fancy them on a bike either with all this traffic around. But then the cars, buses and lorries leave the ancient route and veer off north towards the Via Appia Nuova, a crowded modern highway, the familiar SS7.

After the Alban Hills, Appius's engineers drove through the swampy, malarial plain known as the Pontine Marshes, running to Tarracina (Terracina), now a pleasant seaside tourist town on the coast. Here I saw for myself just how straight a line he and his team could draw. Above Terracina sits a vast temple complex dedicated to Jupiter Anxur. It's a struggle to find, especially when your satnav guides you to the exact geographical location for the place *directly in the road tunnel which runs beneath it.* Thanks for that, TomTom.

I did eventually make my way to the hilltop above, along a vertiginous narrow road. The temple is so huge it's hard to appreciate the scale and complexity of everything close up. But the views... looking back towards Rome a ruler-like tree-lined avenue cuts a perfect diagonal into the town. Unmistakably Appian. Track back a few miles along the SS7 and there's some of the most picturesque driving anywhere on this journey, the road running dead straight for mile after mile beneath the cover of stone pines dotted in perfect symmetry along the verge.

After Tarracina geology intervened, making Appius's goal of a straight line impossible because of the rocky coastline. The forced labour – local peasants as far as we know – made cuttings and embankments through sheer rock to run parallel with the coastline to Formia and Minturnae (Minturno), then south to the lost town of Sinuessa before turning inland for the final stretch to Capua.

In all, this first section of Appius's marvel stretched to 132 miles, across terrain that varied from the soft volcanic tuff of Rome to swamp and hard mountain rock. His engineers and the anonymous crews who sweated over the task had to drain marshes, excavate through steep cliffs, and construct bridges across rivers. For all that they are thought to have completed the entire length into Capua within the space of five years. You can't help but wonder what the Samnites, who could never have countenanced such a task, must have thought.

The modern Via Appia mutates from fast highway to impassable rural track all along its length. Narrow, potholed lanes run past little shops, farms and restaurants, indistinguishable from any other road in rural Italy. Then there are the few preserved stretches of neat, polished cobblestones, sometimes large, sometimes small, which are essentially restored archaeological exhibits.

For the most part, both Appius's original route, from Rome to Capua, and its later extensions, to Beneventum then on to Tarentum (Taranto) and Brundisium (Brindisi), are either buried under a modern highway like the SS7, or else, especially in the little-populated wilds of Basilicata, gone altogether. We can find remarkable proof of the latter in Campania on the SS7 just past the village of Castello del Lago. Here a side track leads to the ruins of a bridge known as the Ponte Rotto (broken bridge), marooned in a sea of broad, open farm fields. This was once a proud feature of the Via Appia, a seven or eight-arch bridge across the broad waters of the Calore. Now the river is little more than a stream. There's no sign of the remains of a road in either direction, though if you scan the site through the satellite view in something like

Google Maps you just might be able to guess where the old highway ran.

This is the reality for anyone like me who dreamed of following the Via Appia its entire length. It's impossible on foot – no one would want to walk a busy highway like the SS7. Pretty much impractical by scooter, bicycle or car too. Though it only took me a couple of days to realise this didn't matter anyway. The story of Appius's creation is a narrative about people, places and the effect they had on their world and ours. It's a tale about building a civilisation, much more than just a road, however impressive that highway might be.

Not that Appius Claudius Caecus would recognise a foot of it anywhere. He was trying to build a military support system for Rome's soldiers as quickly and efficiently as he could – which meant that his first version would have been finished with gravel, not those handsome geometric Sampietrini cobblestones we see in the historic parts today. Only later did engineers create the complex, multi-layer road bed eleven yards wide or so, with drainage at the sides to keep it usable during heavy rains, that would carry the weight of soldiers and travellers for centuries.

Appius was planning for battle, and he was going to get it.

❧ 3 ☙

THE ROAD TO WAR

IT'S NOT hard to fall in love with Campania. The coast is the stuff of painters' dreams, from the glorious sweep of the Bay of Naples to the Amalfi coast and the islands – Capri, Ischia – where Hollywood stars now moor their boats and dine in restaurants where one cocktail costs the price of a whole meal elsewhere. Much as rich Romans did two millennia before.

Inland, this is one of the richest agricultural regions of Italy, famous for fruit and vegetables, wine, meat and cheese. The Romans and the Samnites wouldn't have known what to do with that Campanian staple of today, the tomato, since it didn't arrive in Italy from Peru until the sixteenth century. But you don't have to be in Campania long to understand why everyone from the Greeks and Normans to the Spanish and French have cast a covetous eye at a region the Romans dubbed 'Campania Felix', happy countryside.

As the engineers drove the Via Appia south, Rome's neighbours began to understand that they were dealing with a pugnacious state fast acquiring a thirst for territory: theirs. Either cities acquiesced and became craven satellites or faced violent and bloody occupation. That said, Rome never set out to occupy the whole of Italy, let alone the rest of the Mediterranean and beyond. The various officers of the state, senators, consuls, generals, picked off territories piece by piece, usually after an argument, perhaps one that had been provoked. With each new possession came another horizon... and before long the Via Appia was to provide one of the most tempting.

THE YEARS Appius was building his road were marked by constant campaigning against both the Samnites in the south and the Etruscans to the north. In 304 BC the Second Samnite War, which began twenty-three years earlier, when Rome had tried to create colonies in Campania around Neapolis, came to an end with the Samnites suing for peace. Six years on the two sides were at each other's throats again. One year later the final massed battle began.

Rome's enemies had pooled forces, Samnites, Etruscans, Umbrians and the Celtic Gauls known as the Senone from the north coming together at Sentinum, outside modern Sassoferrato in the Marche. The dispute that had flared at the Caudine Forks now engrossed most of Italy. It was probably the largest concerted enemy coalition Rome had ever faced. Two very different commanders led the Roman forces, the cautious Quintus Fabius and the decidedly more aggressive Publius Decius Mus, a man from a military family and proud of it. The Etruscans and the Umbrians were drawn away into another engagement and then, with roughly equal forces, battle was joined. The wary Fabius held back in defence. Decius, eager for action, went on the attack. It failed and soon his lines were broken by enemy chariots and infantry.

At that point, says Livy, Decius lost it and cried out, 'Why am I delaying the fate of my family any longer?' This was no spur-of-the-moment madness. Decius was about to follow a ritual known as 'devotio' in which a general gave his life to the gods in return for victory. His father, also Publius Decius Mus, perished the same way when fighting Samnites and other enemy forces on the slopes of Vesuvius in 340 BC. There were prayers, rituals, then he put on the same kind of armour worn by his father and uttered a chilling warning, 'I carry before me terror and rout and carnage and blood and the wrath of all the gods, those above and those below. I will infect the standards, the armour, the weapons of the enemy with dire and manifold death. The place of my destruction shall also witness that of the Gauls and Samnites.'

After which he charged headlong into the midst of the opposing ranks where the Samnites took him down with arrows since no man fancied fighting him in person. Nineteen years later Decius's son, another Publius Decius Mus, was in the thick of another battle as the Romans fought the Pyrrhic Wars to seize control of the whole of southern Italy, extending the Via Appia to Tarentum. Decius Junior, it seems, was hellbent on following dad and granddad with his own act of 'devotio' and, depending on which historian you believe, managed it. Funnily enough the name 'Publius Decius Mus' vanishes from the chronicles at this point.

Back on the field at Sentinum, the gods appeared to be listening. Decius's troops rallied after the heroic death of their general. Fabius pounced, and Rome finished the bloody day victorious, with 8,700 of its own dead against 20,000 of its enemy. This was the effective end not only of the third and final Samnite war, but of the Samnites too.

Appius was a player in Rome by now. He'd already been consul and, after the victory at Sentinum, he was given Decius's surviving troops to mop up the remnants of the Samnite army hiding out around Beneventum and beyond. The balance of power in Italy had clearly shifted. While rebel groups would appear from time to time – really they never went away – mainland Italy, from Umbria to much of the south, was now in the hands of Rome.

When the soldiers' job was done, the road builders began work. Before long the thirty miles of road from Capua to Beneventum was completed and the bridge that was so hard to find driven across the Sabato river. Looking at the exhibits so lovingly displayed in the Benevento museum, and all the local history books devoted to studies of Samnite culture, I could only wonder what old Herennius would have said if he was still around. This was the end of the Samnites' world, their language, their culture, their identity. Not that the Romans needed to outlaw it. They were, above all, practical conquerors and simply demanded that people who wished to deal with them should do so on their terms, in their way and, eventually, in their language too.

Herennius's warning – 'Whatever this disgrace burns into their souls will rankle there forever, and allow them no rest till they've made you pay for it many times over' – had come true. His son Pontius who'd ignored it wasn't there to offer an apology. He'd been captured in battle and executed some years before on the orders of that same Quintus Fabius, the hero of Sentinum.

The defeated regions of Italy were forced into alliances. Any rebels who held out were hunted down and slaughtered. Within a few years Rome had reached Venusia (Venosa) in Lucania, an important stopping point on the Via Appia for centuries to come. The way south surely beckoned, though it brought with it unknown difficulties. By subduing their neighbouring city states, Rome had taken control of most of Italy inhabited by what they might think of as their people, Italic tribes sharing similar languages and customs. The far south would bring this noisy infant empire face to face with a different world altogether.

DRIVING EAST from Benevento I found myself travelling ever further from the Italy I'd come to know over decades, the sophisticated, international cities of Rome and Florence, Venice and Naples. The cornucopia of Campania falls away and in its place rises the harsher landscape of Basilicata. There are vines aplenty, but none of the great swathes of green I'd seen so far. From time to time I would pass a field where tomatoes sprawl in untidy rows, figures bent between them picking at the fruit. Perhaps locals, happy to be working. Or immigrant labour under the thumb of hard gang masters. That can of tomatoes may be cheap when it hits the supermarket but there are places where people have paid for it in ways not so distant from the tied, agricultural slaves who once worked the country estates for rich Roman masters. They will have their turn in this story too, and soon.

Before long I'm taking the winding road marked for Venosa and, after navigating a flock of stray dogs that seem to want to wag their tail at everyone who visits, I find myself headed into a small town with a big past. Rome, with its noise and hectic pace and gridlock, is more than 200 miles away. Venosa is such a soporific, welcoming place I have to resist the temptation to put down roots for more time than I can spare. There's a downside to this sleepiness, though. The Romans may have poured resources and people into Venosa, around 20,000 newcomers or so as it built the place up as a border stronghold. But modern Basilicata is the region of mainland Italy that's been hit hardest by rural depopulation. There's been a steady drift away from low-paid agricultural work towards the cities for years. Of late that's turned into a flood, so much that some villages have come up with imaginative schemes to reverse the trend.

Immigrants from Africa, shunned in some parts of the country, particularly the north, have been welcomed as a means to rebuild the local economy. In the village of Grottole to the south, where six hundred homes lie empty and the population has shrunk to two thousand, the American giant Airbnb is paying for a handful of foreign visitors to stay for three months in the hope of building up the tourist trade. Given how many locals have been priced out of their homes by Airbnb in cities throughout Europe, this is, perhaps, little more than a PR exercise. But desperate people take whatever they can get.

Venosa doesn't look on its uppers, at least not yet. The population of around 12,000 – less than in Roman times – is relatively stable. The town also benefits from being at the heart of the Vulture region – from the nearby extinct volcano, Monte Vulture, not the bird – with its popular red wine based on the Aglianico grape. All the same, there's the distinct feeling of somewhere on the edge of neglect. The local train station closed a few years back and is now just a derelict building next to a rusty track at the edge of town. When I drove out to leave, the satnav guided me down a road that ended in potholes, mud and chaos.

For the visitor looking for the proverbial off-the-beaten-track Italy, it's a find. When I turned up houses throughout the town were festooned with ribbons of bright red, pointed sweet peppers, dried here to make a local speciality known as *peperone crusco*. These are then fried in oil to make them crispy and used in a variety of dishes. The old town comprises a long, winding cobbled street, at one end a petrol station and beyond that the archaeological area, most of what's left of the Roman settlement. At the other lies the squat, rather ugly fifteenth-century Aragonese castle, now a civic museum, surrounded by a dry moat. Here, on one side, runs a line of cafes where locals gather of an evening.

Venusia proved so strategically crucial to Rome's ambitions that it rapidly turned into a 'statio', the ancient equivalent of a motorway service station, though with a few extras you won't find at Watford Gap today. On the scorching September afternoon I visited the archaeological area, there were just two other people meandering through the excavated 'statio' that accommodated travellers on the Via Appia for centuries. At first sight it might appear one more set of ruins among so many, though this one sits next to the slightly less ruined Abbey of Santissima Trinità, a Norman church that replaced earlier Christian buildings and before them a temple devoted to Hymen. Closer up the mosaics and the complexity of the Roman area tell a more convoluted story.

BY THE TIME the Via Appia reached Venusia it was three decades or so old. A generation was growing up that took it for granted they had access to a fast, direct way to travel in and out of Rome, one that was getting longer and better the more Rome's territory grew. Cobbles were going down to cover the gravel surface worn away with the busy traffic, all cambered so that the rain ran off into the drainage ditches built on each side to the careful specifications of a new generation of engineers. Over the years formal arrangements for maintenance would come into force, officials deputed to make sure the road was kept in good condition at public expense, though with some local contributions. And woe betide anyone that allowed an important consular road such as the Appia to fall into disrepair.

When he was censor, raiding the treasury to pay for his pet project, Appius saw it as an aid to the military in their fight against the Samnites, a way of turning Capua into a front line hub for the battles to come. But while it may have been a road for the military, it wasn't a military road. Anyone could use it so long as they paid the occasional toll, for bridges for example, along with tariffs on goods. As the bureaucracy of the Roman state began to grow, more and more the roads were used for official correspondence, news and bulletins to the front. For tourism, too. Aristocrats wanting to escape the vicious summer heat of Rome could head off from the Porta Capena and be in the cool, green forests around the lakes of Albano and Nemi in a day. They would travel by closed wagon, two of which could pass each other abreast without a problem. Farmers would use horse-drawn carts to ship their fruit, vegetables and meat from the rich farmland around Aricia, spend the night in a tavern or brothel in the big, bad city if they felt like it, and be back home the following evening. Villagers who might never have expected to see Rome in their lifetime came to find there were good reasons, economic and practical, to make a journey beyond the reach of their fathers.

As anyone who's watched modern road building knows, creating new motorways and expanding existing ones rarely solves traffic problems. It simply encourages more people to fill the empty space that's suddenly available. The same happened with the Romans and their innovative new highway from north to south. You certainly got out of the way if a legion of soldiers was marching down there, but after that the highway was yours. Rome was discovering that roads didn't simply allow troops to move swiftly to battle. They generated trade, money, and people, lots of them demanding services as they passed, food, accommodation, fresh horses and entertainment.

The Via Appia ran right through the archaeological area of today's Venosa, bringing with it floods of wayfarers and their cash. This is the complex of buildings that sprang up over the centuries to cater for them. There are houses, two rather swish, others more ordinary. A public bath sits in the middle of the complex, with the underfloor heating system still visible and an elegant mosaic floor. Across the modern road is a small amphitheatre, for both dramatic productions and gladiatorial contests. Not that it was open while I was there – I suspect there wasn't the staff.

That would not have been a problem a couple of millennia ago.

Here, anyone on the move could find whatever they wanted – food, baths, entertainment, and a bed for the night.

There would also be company, drinking companions, brothels and pimps. For evidence of that we only need to return to our poet friend Horace. He was born in Venusia in 65 BC, its most famous citizen ahead of Carlo Gesualdo, prince of the town, who, in 1590, slaughtered his wife and her lover after catching them in bed together, got away with it because he was a noble, and spent the rest of his life doing little else but writing weird and melancholy madrigals.

Carlo spent very little time in Venosa. Horace – Orazio to the Italians – left at an early age as well, but would return on his travels and pined after his pretty, bucolic home from time to time in verse. You'll find a small building labelled 'The House of Horace' in the older part of town; unfortunately there is no typographic character which says 'take this with a very large grain of salt', which is perhaps just as well because it might be overused in this story. Around the corner in the handsome square named after the chap, the Piazza Orazio Flacco, you can enjoy a pleasant breakfast or snack in the Caffè Centrale by a statue of the poet.

He looks very grand in his toga and wreath, but don't be fooled: Horace was quite the lad. He left us an interesting record of a journey along the Via Appia in the form of a poem, Satire 1.5, describing a trip he made from Rome to Brundisium during the 30s BC in famous company. On the journey he meets his beloved friend and fellow poet, Virgil, in the company of the political power player Maecenas, the right-hand man of Octavian, the emperor-to-be Augustus. It's a fascinating and cryptic narrative of a journey that comes across as a poetical account of a jolly chaps' business jaunt with some entertainment on the side. Horace describes an evening event somewhere between Benevento and his home town.

Here, like an idiot, I stay awake in the middle of the night waiting for the lying girl to come; eager for some action, damned sleep overcomes me; then wet dreams swamp my night clothes and soil my belly.

That is my rough, free and unpoetic translation. But I can assure you it's a sight closer to the original than anything you'll find in most school textbooks, or the older translations of Horace which were often the work of Victorian-era clergymen. Unless Horace had a lover in every 'statio' along the Via Appia, the 'lying girl' was a prostitute hired for the night who, perhaps, found a better-paying customer. Though there's more to be said about Horace's curious journey, which is not quite what it seems, later in this tale.

THIS, then, was life developing along the road – rough and ready and real. After a delightful day exploring this engaging little town I took a drink among the locals outside the Aragonese castle then wandered into the old town looking for food. Venosa boasts a fancy restaurant, *L'Incanto*, that everyone seems to rave about for its local dishes. But on my own an eight-course tasting menu seemed a bit much so instead I head past Orazio's statue for the hotel named after him and sit down to home-made *fusilli alla Lucana* – made with those peperone crusco – fillet of pork with liquorice potatoes, fresh fruit and a glass of Aglianico. One day I'll be back in Venosa and for more than a single night.

That wine gives a clue about where we're headed. It used to be called Ellenico – Greek. One of the oldest varieties known, thought to have been brought to Italy by the settlers of *Magna Graecia*, Greater Greece. Colonies that had emigrated there from across the Ionian sea centuries before, establishing communities that were variously famed for trade, for luxury, philosophy and early science. They weren't wandering tribes of mountain shepherds, without much in the way of government, strategy or learning. Rome's next enemy was smart, educated and bemused by the idea that an upstart from the north could even think of casting hungry glances at its rich and sophisticated cities. Like the Samnites at the Caudine Forks, they could not have been reading matters more dangerously wrong.

As Rome was integrating northern Lucania into its portfolio of conquered territories, a boy called Archimedes was born across the sea in the Greek city of Syracusae (Siracusa). He was destined to become one of the foremost scientists of his time, a writer and inventor who, among so much else, easily confirmed the earth was round centuries before a few bright sparks in the Catholic Church decided it wasn't. A genius who six decades or so later would die on the sword of a soldier taking the most important Greek city in Sicily for Rome.

And here, as I read and read, thinking about what I'd seen, came one of those moments that sends a shiver up the spine. A connection across cultures and centuries that suddenly leaps out at you from the past. Wandering around the town earlier, ticking off what few sights there are, I'd ambled down a slightly scruffy street called Via Madonna della Scala. There, opposite what looks like a derelict house and an abandoned building site, sits a pile of stones cemented together, protected behind iron railings, not that you'd think they were needed. This, the local tourist map indicated, was all that was left of the tomb of Marcus Claudius Marcellus, once a consul of Rome but, let's face it, with two a year and centuries to fill there are an awful lot of them.

Idling at my table between courses, wondering where I could buy a bottle of the wonderful olive oil to take home, I looked him up. Rome had a lot of toffs with that name over the centuries but it wasn't hard to nail down this one. Five times consul, he was also one of their most famous generals, so fearsome in battle he came to be known as 'the Sword of Rome', one of only three recognised winners of the highest award any Roman general could attain, the *spolia opima,* the 'rich spoils' awarded for killing an enemy general in single combat. That was for slaying a Gallic king in the north in 225 BC. Later, during the Second Punic War against Carthage, he commanded forces in Sicily, alongside a chap called Appius Claudius Pulcher, grandson of the same Appius who kicked all this off with his plan for a new road. Then it comes in a flash so quick I nearly spit out my lovely glass of Venosa wine. While there Marcellus led the forces that stormed the Greek city of Syracusae, murdering everyone they found, plundering its fabled riches. Among the slaughtered was poor Archimedes, a death Marcellus was said to regret.

Four years later, in 208 BC, he was named consul for the fifth and final time and went to take charge of the forces at Venusia. There he went out with a band of two hundred and twenty cavalry to reconnoitre what they believed was unoccupied territory. They were ambushed by a superior force of Hannibal's men and the Sword of Rome died fighting in the field. Supposedly Hannibal gave him a hero's funeral, then sent his ashes back in a silver urn, presumably into that crooked pile of weather-beaten stones now trapped in cement in the Via Madonna della Scala. There, right in front of me, was history linking fingers across the centuries, something that was to happen on this trip time and time again.

When the Romans were first garrisoning Venusia the Carthaginian general Hannibal lay in the future. They were focused on more immediate targets. Beyond the bare hills of Lucania lay the heel of Italy with tempting access to ports that offered rich possibilities for both trade and yet more military adventures. The most obvious route forward would lead them to Tarentum (Taranto), a city with great wealth, formidable resources and little regard for Rome. A place that was home to the most fiery and pugnacious Greek tribe of all, the Spartans.

ENTER THE GREEKS

ROMANS ALWAYS LOVED the story of their city's foundation and still do when they celebrate that annual 'birthday' on April 21st with a popular historical parade. The legend goes back to the Trojan War – probably in the 11th or 12th century BC. It claims that Aeneas, son of the Trojan prince Anchises and the goddess Aphrodite, fled the burning ruins of his home in Asia Minor and, after various adventures, sailed to central Italy. There, following the inevitable local war, he founded the coastal city of Latium, somewhere between modern Anzio and Ostia and a family line that would, unknown generations in the future, include Romulus and Remus. The Julian clan – the most famous member being, of course, Julius Caesar – claimed to be descended directly from Aeneas which meant they weren't just in the bloodline of a great historic hero but that of a goddess too – Aphrodite, Venus to the Romans. They certainly seemed to think they were divine at times.

However true this origin story may be – there's a call for that 'grain of salt' typographic character again, writ very large and not just about the god bit – it's clear that the Greeks were in southern Italy long before Rome existed as a functioning city. They loved the sweep of the Bay of Naples, settling first in Cumae then building Neapolis. That had been lost to the Romans before the final Samnite war began. But elsewhere there were large, powerful and wealthy Greek cities in Sicily, in Tarentum and Brundisium just forty miles away, as well as several smaller settlements too.

To call them colonies was a misnomer. When the Romans pinched territory from someone else and created a settlement, it was clear where the boss was – at the end of one of the consular roads that led to back to the Capitoline Hill. In Magna Graecia, each new unit looked not to Greece as its homeland but one of the many city states across the sea. Some, such as Brundisium, were home to a population that spoke Greek, followed Greek cultural ways, but felt attached to no one at all.

Even if the parental bonds were strong, there was a long and sometimes perilous sea crossing between the homeland and its Italian offspring, quite an obstacle if they felt threatened. Then there was the way the progeny behaved once they'd flown the nest which was all too often like teenagers allowed on their first 18-30 holiday to Benidorm. The abundant agricultural lands of Italy and Sicily offered riches that were unavailable back home. Before long some of the Magna Graecia colonies became so affluent they adopted hedonistic lifestyles that horrified traditionalists. The Greek philosopher Empedocles was supposed to have said of his home city Akragas (Agrigento) in Sicily, 'The Akragantinians make merry as if they must die tomorrow, and build as if they would live forever'. Though since he went on to commit suicide by throwing himself into the fiery crater of Etna, in part to prove some philosophical point, it must be admitted he was never the life and soul of any party.

Greece excelled at sending out ships of marauding warriors – or 'heroes' as they'd call them – to rape and pillage and steal the land of others. But turning those newly won territories into a connected, established empire under central control was quite beyond the ragtag collection of bickering cities back home. Only one Greek of note had set out on a concerted journey of global conquest and that was Alexander the Great who'd left his home of Macedon, wandered the Middle East as far as India, conquering as he saw fit then moving on when he got bored, only to fall fatally ill in Babylon at the age of 32.

Alexander's vast empire was unravelling even as he died in 323 BC, possibly of poison, just before our story begins at the Caudine Forks. The legacy he left behind was substantial – including the great Egyptian city named after him, Alexandria, where he was laid to rest in a grand sarcophagus after his corpse was seized on its way back to Macedon. Hellenistic influence continued for centuries throughout Africa and Asia Minor, notably in the line of Ptolemies who ruled Egypt for nearly three hundred years. The first Ptolemy was one of Alexander's bodyguards from Macedon. Greek, not Egyptian, would continue to be the official language of government until the Ptolemies fell with the suicide of Cleopatra and the murder of her son with Julius Caesar, Caesarion. Quite an achievement but Alexander's legacy was nothing like a functioning empire, any more than the colonies of Magna Graecia were genuine, connected outposts of their mother cities back in Greece.

The city of Tarentum, rich, hedonistic, blessed with one of the finest harbours in southern Italy, and in temperament somewhat removed from its ascetic, Spartan forebears, was a cultured place of theatre, science and philosophy. What did clever folk like these have to fear from a bunch of upstart, unkempt northerners fresh from trouncing a tribe of nomads wandering the bare hills with a few sheep?

VENOSA TO TARANTO was around two hours by car, with the route of the original Via Appia pretty much lost or hidden most of the way. It certainly ran to the picturesque small town of Gravina then on to Altamura. Afterwards it skirted Basilicata's biggest new tourist hotspot, Matera, famous for its cave hotels which are probably the only places in the world where a room without a view costs more than one with. They were filming a James Bond movie in Matera while I was there so the place was full of film people and paparazzi. Knowing the curious mix of mayhem and boredom that comes with the process of making a movie, I kept the nose of the Abarth pointed at the southern horizon.

I had to get to Taranto. It's too important a stop on the journey of the Via Appia to shirk in spite of all the warnings I'd received. When I told a friend from Venice I was headed there he took a deep breath and said, 'It's OK so long as you don't drink the water or breathe the air.' Then I read a modern-day Horace bleating on TripAdvisor that it was the dirtiest, most polluted, unpleasant and crime-ridden city in Italy, especially in the centre. After that, naturally, I immediately booked a hotel slap bang in the middle. This was one of the glories of Magna Graecia. Surely there had to be something left?

Not much. Taranto's ideal location as a commercial harbour turned out to be its modern undoing. The vast steel works of Ilva dominate the city and provide most of its jobs, at no small cost. Pollution levels are dreadful with deaths from lung cancer thirty per cent higher than elsewhere in Italy, and mortality from serious respiratory disease in men fifty per cent higher. To the north the stink of burning coke is appalling while a fine and poisonous dust falls day and night. But traces of the ancient city are still there on the island that's the Old Town sitting between the Ionian Sea looking over towards Calabria and the huge inland lagoon known as the Mare Piccolo or Little Sea.

It's a chaotic, rundown spot, reminiscent of a crumpled version of Spaccanapoli, Naples' seedy but historic arterial area, itself based around an old Roman main street. Cramped winding lanes of crumbling buildings, some once palatial, some decidedly not, run higgledy-piggledy across the little island to no discernible pattern. Parking's a nightmare and I feared for the little car when I finally found a spot to leave her. As I checked into my hotel the receptionist gave me an explanation how a huge renovation project is planned for the entire island, her way of saying, I suspect, 'It will get better, honest.' Before that she'd quickly relocked the front door to keep out the beggar pestering everyone in the street. Duly welcomed, I ventured out in the hope of finding something, anything of historic note.

After a few minutes a persistent pensioner wearing a city badge came out and beckoned me to a doorway. Much of ancient Taranto still lies underground in 'ipogei', underground chambers, some dating back to Greek times, others more recent. For the next half hour I was treated to a personal tour of three of the nearest, all spotlessly renovated by the city, beautifully lit, handsome to look at and with nothing by way of explanation. Quite fascinating if a little short on detail.

At the end my genial guide looked up and asked, 'Coffee?'

'Thanks,' I answered, thinking what a generous place this was. 'Just had one.'

'No. I meant for me.'

She was a charming old lady, full of life, though her heavily accented Italian wasn't easy to follow. Well worth a tip even if I wasn't quite sure what exactly I'd just visited. Above ground there's little Greek or Roman to see except two Doric columns from a temple standing in open ground on the Via Duomo. Across the iron swing bridge that links the Old Town to the modern centre sits a well-organised and substantial archaeological museum with a huge collection of exhibits, many quite remarkable, dating through Roman to Spartan times and before. This was the residential and commercial area for ordinary locals when Taranto was Tarentum, as we'll come to see.

When I turned up the museum seemed so short of staff that the few visitors it had couldn't move from floor to floor until an attendant could be found to take you there. Waiting thirty minutes before you can visit parts of a large museum is a new one on me. Apparently the place was affected by the financial crisis engulfing the city council. Beyond the museum and the *ipogei* there's little to attract tourists during the day to be honest. But it's a different place of an evening when the *centro storico* comes alive with cafes, bars, music and restaurants. A bohemian crowd turns up to enjoy the night, the food is excellent, and I finally begin to warm to the place even if it never quite loses that industrial tang in the air.

With a little work and some imagination, the extensive statuary and ceramics in the city museum and those underground chambers do give you some appreciation of what Rome was taking on when it put ancient Tarentum next on its hit list. You just pine for a glimpse of the beautiful, hedonistic city that was once here. One day when all that money's spent on the Old Town I may return. For now, I was glad the Abarth was still sitting there untouched the next morning.

One night was enough, and it's worth remembering this is only a one-hour train ride from lovely Brindisi. A fleeting visit may well suffice.

The Romans planned to stay much longer.

In March 1939 Hitler's troops entered Czechoslovakia, ostensibly to protect the interests of threatened German citizens there. The Second World War rapidly followed.

The old 'they asked us for help' gambit is one that states have used for millennia to spark a conflict they want to happen but only if they can claim the other side gave them an excuse. Then there are the so-called 'false flag' incidents where some kind of outrage is faked to generate a desired response, like the Reichstag fire and the Mukden incident, a fire started by the Japanese to draw them into an invasion of Manchuria.

Did something like this happen with Rome and Tarentum? Perhaps. Tensions were rising between the two after Rome defeated the Samnites and began to garrison Venusia, too close to Tarentum for comfort. The Greek historian Appian of Alexandria (no relation to Appius the road builder) takes up the story. In 282 BC he has a fleet of ten Roman ships, full of troops 'sight-seeing' – the way troop ships do – along the Ionian coast. They were probably on their way to support Thurii, a small Greek colony south of the city. To the Tarentines' disgust, Thurii had come out for Rome and allowed a garrison of their troops to be stationed there.

Tarentum really didn't appreciate the Romans sailing warships across their bay, something they claimed broke a treaty of which the Romans appeared to be ignorant. According to one account, wine had been liberally taken as part of one of their many festivals. As furious as they were drunk, they sent out their own ships, sank four of the Roman vessels and captured the rest. The leader of the unfortunate Roman fleet, Publius Cornelius Dolabella, had been consul the year before and either drowned or was slaughtered, along with lots of others.

The Romans sent one of their toffs, Lucius Postumius Megellus, to give Tarentum a good talking to. No one liked Megellus much. He'd been consul three times and was widely regarded as arrogant and crooked. But he'd overseen the capture of Venusia, so perhaps he was just the most senior man in the area for the job.

Megellus duly turned up in Tarentum as an ambassador and addressed a public meeting, demanding the return of all surviving Roman prisoners 'taken, not in war, but as mere sight-seers' and the handover of the locals who'd been responsible for sinking the ships and killing those on board. He addressed the public assembly in Greek – badly, which the Tarentines thought highly amusing. Trying to impress, Megellus also wore a toga with a purple stripe, which they found equally hilarious. No chap in Tarentum would have been seen dead in a bath robe. Real men all wore skirts.

Then, to add to their mirth, one of the locals walked up and peed on him while he was pontificating. As the hall rocked with laughter a stony-faced Megellus said, 'You lot are going to wash this out with gouts of blood – I trust you enjoyed the joke.'

Not long after dispatching the Roman embassy north, empty-handed apart from a furious former consul's pee-stained toga, the Tarentines sobered up and thought, 'Oops.' Then they made the equivalent of a 999 call across the Ionian to a chap who was a second cousin of Alexander the Great and quite convinced he was cut from the late hero's same cloth: Pyrrhus, king of an obscure Greek tribe who sound as if they came out of an early episode of Star Trek, the Molossians.

When Pyrrhus took the call from Tarentum he'd already established himself as the kind of chap who, if he'd been Glaswegian, would have cruised every Gorbals bar on a Saturday night hunting for the one with the best fight. In his three decades he'd been on and off the throne of Epirus a few times, served as a mercenary, married the step-daughter of Ptolemy I, Alexander's old bodyguard, now running Egypt, sat as co-ruler of Epirus only to murder his fellow king, start a war against his brother-in-law, then share the throne of Macedon for a while until his co-regent forced him out.

Plutarch, in his life of Pyrrhus, seems to have the measure of the man when he reports that, when one of his sons, by different mothers, asked which of them was going to inherit the kingdom he replied, 'Whichever of you keeps his sword the sharpest.'

Just to make sure everyone got the message, Plutarch added...

...he thought it tedious to the point of nausea if he were not inflicting mischief on others or suffering it at others' hands, and like Achilles could not endure idleness, 'but ate his heart away, remaining there, and pined for war-cry and battle'.

Stuck in Epirus, kicking his heels, in his mid-thirties, older than his more famous cousin when he expired after conquering much of the known world, Pyrrhus was fretting about where the next punch-up was coming from when the message from Tarentum came in: *Save us from the Romans and this city is yours.*

MODERN TARANTO MIGHT NOT LOOK the most enticing prospect for a territory-hungry adventurer. It certainly didn't for me wandering its grubby and largely deserted streets. But take in a satellite view on something like Google Maps and you start to see what might have brought Pyrrhus running across the Ionian, anxious for a fight. Blank out all the industrial dross and you'll see a fine outer harbour, the second secure inner one of the Mare Piccolo and that island strategically placed to defend both. From its position on the inner heel of Italy, Tarentum was well placed for shipping, east to Greece, then south west to Calabria and Sicily. Trade meant power and money, and Pyrrhus coveted both.

He was an eccentric but no fool, and quite the general when called upon. He also had an adviser he greatly admired, Cineas, a chap, he said, who'd won him more cities with his eloquence than he had with his armies. When Cineas heard of the plan to take on the Romans, he took Pyrrhus to one side and asked... is this really wise? What next?

After Tarentum and the defeat of Rome then the rest of Italy, Pyrrhus replied.

And after that? Cineas wondered.

Sicily.

And after *that?*

Libya and Carthage. By which time no one in the world would dare mock Pyrrhus and his empire, and they could all sit down, have a good drink and natter and relax. Cineas took a deep breath and pointed out they could all have a good drink and natter and relax already, but Pyrrhus wasn't listening. Soon he set sail for Tarentum with three thousand horse, twenty thousand infantry, two thousand archers, five hundred slingers and, a loan from his chums in Egypt, a secret weapon the Romans had never yet encountered: twenty elephants.

THE TARENTINES WERE HAPPY, but not for long. They'd become accustomed to a life of luxury, with wine, women, song, theatre and public exhibitions. In short they were sybaritic, which is appropriate since the word comes from an equally hedonistic place called Sybaris, a Greek colony that once prospered where awkward Thurii sat down the coast.

Pyrrhus, much as he professed to long for the quiet life, a chat with friends and good wine, was very much of the opinion all that had to wait. It was time to be serious, not for party games.

Plutarch again...

...he closed the gymnasia and the public areas where, as they strolled about, they told each other old war stories; he also put a stop to the drinking-bouts, revels, and festivals as unseasonable, called the men to arms, and was stern and inexorable in his enrolment of them for military service.

This was not the deal the Tarentines thought they'd struck. They were Spartan by heritage, not by nature, and a good many left the city to find somewhere the bars were still open.

In 280 BC Pyrrhus met the Romans on the plain near Heraclea, a Greek town close to what is now the quiet seaside resort of Policoro, south west of Tarentum. It was a close-fought battle until Pyrrhus turned loose his twenty elephants, panicking the Roman horse and soldiers alike. After that the northerners turned tail and fled, though the losses on both sides were heavy.

Here, one last time, we make the acquaintance of Appius Claudius Caecus, the man who started this story with his raiding of the Roman treasury to build the road that would carry his name. By now he was old, blind – which is what 'caecus' means – and so infirm he had to be carried everywhere. All the same, no one was ever going to shut up Appius when he had something to say. After Heraclea, Pyrrhus had dispatched his right-hand man the persuasive Cineas to Rome with an offer of peace. The Greek was a real charmer and turned up with presents for the senators' wives and toys for their children – all of which were immediately rejected. We're more than two hundred and fifty years away from Virgil, in the Aeneid, warning, 'Beware Greeks bearing gifts'. But it seems his predecessors had the idea already. After putting away his presents, Cineas came up with an offer. Pyrrhus would release all his Roman prisoners without ransom and even help Rome subjugate the rest of Italy. All the Greek king wanted in return was immunity for Tarentum.

A reluctant and cowed Senate, perhaps thinking of those giant grey elephants, creatures out of fantasy, bearing down on their city, was about to fold and agree a peace when Appius heard and had his relatives carry him into the assembly. There he made a stirring speech that would resonate with Romans for centuries to come. Plutarch reports part of it went like this...

Up to this time, O Romans, I have regarded the misfortune to my eyes as an affliction, but it now distresses me that I am not deaf as well as blind, that I might not hear the shameful resolutions and decrees of years which bring low the glory of Rome... Don't suppose you'll rid yourself of this fellow by making him your friend. No, you'll bring others against you and they will despise you as men whom anybody can easily subdue if Pyrrhus goes away without being punished for his insults, but actually rewarded for them in letting Tarentines and Samnites mock the Romans.

The Senate was always up for a good speech, and this was one of the best. They would perhaps have been naive to accept Pyrrhus's promise of peace in any case; as he would have been if he'd believed theirs. Fired up by Appius, they told Cineas to go back to his master and tell him to get out of Italy first and then talk peace. And if he stayed to expect they'd fight him with all their might, whatever the cost, however long it took.

A brief period of polite diplomacy followed. The Romans sent back a future senator, Gaius Fabricius Luscinus, with the disappointed Cineas and tasked him to negotiate the release of Roman prisoners. Fabricius was a highly regarded noble but poor – or at least poor for an aristocrat. Pyrrhus tried to bribe him, to no avail. Then came threats, then philosophical arguments about good and evil. Later, when Fabricius was consul back in Rome, he received a letter from one of Pyrrhus's doctors offering to poison the stubborn Greek king in return for an end to the war. Fabricius simply wrote to Pyrrhus to warn him of the plot and added, 'It would appear that you're a good judge neither of friends nor of enemies. You'll see, when you read this, that the men you're at war with are honourable and just, while those you trust are unjust and base.'

Hostilities resumed. One year later, Pyrrhus's army and the Romans met again, this time at Asculum in Apulia. Here was where that last Publius Decius Mus, now consul, may or may not have sacrificed himself like his father and grandfather before. He was far from alone. It was another costly win, one that led Pyrrhus to complain, 'If we are victorious in one more battle with the Romans, we shall be utterly ruined.' And there is where the term 'Pyrrhic victory' comes from.

After Asculum two things happened. Pyrrhus received a letter from Sicily begging for help. It offered him control of three rich cities – Agrigentum, Syracusae and Leontini (Lentini) – if he came and fought against the Carthaginians there. At the same time he seemed to be coming to the conclusion that it was never going to be easy to beat the Romans if they always came back for more. By this stage Pyrrhus's Alexander the Great complex seems to have truly taken hold. He went to Sicily, fought and fought, fell out with his allies, won and lost battles. When he turned deeply unpopular there, he returned briefly to Italy for one final meeting with the Romans, this time outside Beneventum, now a true Roman colony.

It was 275 BC, five years after Heraclea. In the meantime Roman forces had been swooping on all the parts of Lucania that had held out against them, seizing territory, increasing their ability to feed their forces up and down the Via Appia more with every passing month. They'd also been thinking about elephants. The sight of gigantic, exotic animals lumbering towards them was no longer new to Roman soldiers. They'd worked out some tactics. One trick up their sleeve was to loose squealing pigs – so-called war pigs – and angry horned rams into their midst since the creatures hated the noise and the vicious little beasts.

The approach at Beneventum was much more crude. The Romans loosed javelins at the oncoming elephants, killing two, then badly wounded a young cub which went berserk, scared the rest of the poor animals and Pyrrhus's advantage was lost. As, very soon, was the battle. The Pyrrhic War was over. Three years later Rome took Tarentum, tore down the defensive walls, pillaged its many art treasures and raided the city coffers. But, after paying a huge indemnity, the city was allowed its independence, on paper at least, for now. And the bars and gymnasia would reopen, getting busier over the decades to come as the Via Appia wound its way down from Venusia to the city by the Mare Piccolo.

ITALY WAS NEVER PEACEFUL, not in the decades that followed the Battle of Beneventum or the centuries to come. There were always local rebellions and wars, some minor, some not. Thanks to the ease of trade and travel brought about by Appius's new road, a different cast of players was coming onto the scene. Ambitious individuals were beginning to look beyond national borders towards the Mediterranean, their imaginations fired by the possibilities the Via Appia was bringing to the Roman world. There were fortunes to be made, battles to be won.

Appius Claudius Caecus died two years before the conclusive battle in the Pyrrhic War at Beneventum, one that might never have taken place without that stirring speech to the Senate following Heraclea. Three of his sons would become consuls so he left more than a crucial road and a leaky aqueduct as his legacy.

Pyrrhus was gone too. Forever seeking one more war, he'd returned to Greece to besiege Sparta itself. As he entered the city a woman threw a roof tile from a house window, knocked him off his horse, and an opportunistic soldier leapt out and chopped off his head. He made a lousy ruler, but Plutarch writes that Hannibal rated him the greatest commander the world had ever seen. The polymath politician Cicero wrote about the way he'd released his Roman captives without ransom as 'thoroughly kingly'. Yet his wars had cost at least 40,000 soldiers their lives, along with countless civilians and a good few individuals he'd picked off as political foes, and left no real legacy at all. Cicero, as we will discover, could be a shaky judge of character at times.

The last leg of this journey beckons, forty miles, today mostly along the same direct route the ancient road took across the flat and open land from the Ionian to the Adriatic. By 244 BC the great port of Brundisium was fully a part of the Roman Republic as a colony. There, by the blue waters of one of the finest natural harbours in Europe, the Via Appia ended, as it still does today.

But the story of how it was to reshape the ancient world has only just begun.

II
THEY MAKE A DESERT
AND CALL IT PEACE

The arena, Santa Maria Capua Vetere.

❧ *5* ❧

THE END OF THE ROAD IS THE BEGINNING

I DROVE INTO BRINDISI WARILY, ending up in the queue for a ferry to Corfu for a while. It's a warren of dusty, narrow streets and dead ends. Where I was headed was technically a seafront pedestrian pavement from which outside traffic is banned. But not if you're staying at the Grande Albergo Internazionale on the Viale Regina Margherita waterfront, a handsome if, in parts, slightly dated pile just a few steps away from where the Via Appia ended.

This is a city where the visitor positively drowns in history, some of it behind the grand doors of the Internazionale itself. For part of the Second World War this hotel was effectively the seat of the Italian government when it fled Rome and the Nazis after declaring an armistice with the invading Allies. The king, Vittorio Emmanuele III, led the government from the grand hotel rooms, negotiating with the Allies about the war against the Germans and a phoney Italian rival government headed by Mussolini in Salò, far north in Brescia. All part of a complex, ambiguous story most people outside Italy barely know.

After the Via Appia was completed, Tarentum to Brundisium was a straightforward, direct journey a traveller on horse could complete within a single day. Today it's much the same, an hour or so by car along a speedy road that follows roughly the same track from the smelly industrial wasteland of Taranto to a delightful coastal city that's still largely off the tourist map.

In political and strategic terms, Appius's heirs were now moving into very different territory. When he was raiding the treasury to build his road to Capua in 312 BC, Rome's horizons stopped at her neighbours, and if military matters hadn't gone her way, perhaps would have stayed there. Half a century later the city state had greater ambitions. Roman forces were steadily taking control of most of Italy, and beginning to cast interested eyes across the sea. Brundisium only made the idea of maritime adventures more tempting. It wasn't just another notch in Rome's belt. Over centuries under Greek control it had turned into an important entrepôt city, a port with a busy commercial fleet, captains and crews who, for a fee, could take passengers along Mediterranean routes they knew very well. Much as it is today, with regular ferries to Greece and Albania dotting the horizon as they edge their way out of the modern harbour.

A marble column and the stump of a second stand atop the steps that lead to the waterfront. They were placed there around the third century AD to mark the end of Rome's best-loved road, all three hundred and fifty odd miles of it. Those monuments weren't just yet more markers of Roman achievement. The empire understood full well what Appius's creation, extended down the spine of Italy, had brought her.

Behind the harbour, the old city of Brindisi is a confusing tangle of narrow alleys, flower-bedecked in places, a little rundown elsewhere. We're firmly in the south now in a city where prosperity sits side-by-side with the grubby reality of neglect. Perhaps to encourage more visitors, the sites are mostly free. I walked up to the terrace of the Palazzina del Belvedere, part museum, part panoramic viewpoint of the harbour, then followed the web of alleys inland to the vast archaeological museum, one of the richest in Italy and pretty much empty. There's a cafe with a garden in the old palace that houses it, and not far away the beautiful circular crusaders' church of San Giovanni al Sepolcro.

By early evening diners were starting to come out to eat in the open square of the Piazza Mercato where the daytime market stalls had turned into restaurant tables. Surrounded by happy gossiping local families, you pick the meat or fish you want from the counter and wait for it to emerge fresh from the kitchen. Brindisi has an open, easy air all of its own. As I wandered back to the Internazionale I found the entire waterfront swamped by a couple of thousand people gathered to watch the launch of the new season's basketball team. Italians never embrace anything without enthusiasm, and so passionate are the locals about this imported sport that they stayed there, seated on the steps beneath the Via Appia's final few yards, all night long.

THAT KIND OF DOGGED AND inquisitive determination was beginning to become apparent in a new and adventurous spirit in the Romans. They'd fought their way here in just sixty eight years since Appius laid the first strip of gravel track to Capua. Back then both Brundisium and Tarentum were effectively foreign states. Now they were under the thumb of Rome, and the lesson Appius had taught the city was rapidly sinking in. A series of new, paved roads began to radiate out from the centre like spokes on a majestic wheel. You can still follow their traces today, the Flaminio, running out from the centre of the city, the Piazza del Popolo; the Salaria that ran across the country to the Adriatic; its near neighbour, the Nomentana, one of my favourite urban roads in Rome for the bus ride out to the beautiful circular mausoleum, built for a daughter of the emperor Constantine.

Before long Rome's roads stretched far beyond Italy. At the empire's peak, its territory ran from Britain as far as the Tigris-Euphrates, through Spain and North Africa, encompassing around fifty thousand miles of roads. All built in the first instance for the military and conquest, but soon used for everything from political messenger services to commerce, the creation of private property empires, evangelism and, for those who could afford it, luxurious tourism.

Around 140 BC Rome would undertake one of its greatest road-building projects of all, a companion highway designed to connect with the sea crossing from Brundisium and create a fast link with the east. The Via Egnatia ran for around seven hundred miles from Dyrrhachium (Durres), across Greece to Thessalonika and Thrace, then on to Byzantium, (later Constantinople, now Istanbul). Rome was beginning to think it could change the world. How much it realised the world would come back to change it in return is hard to tell.

CIRCLING the vast basketball crowd on the harbour front, I found myself a cafe by the water's edge and watched the night traffic sail to and fro, small fishing vessels, a local water taxi service, those great ferries headed south to Greece like the ships of two millennia before. Every famous Roman I could think of would have walked the jetties here, some to study in Athens and Rhodes, others, for adventures in Asia Minor, to diplomatic postings, to wars, foreign and civil, to glory, to ignominy, to their deaths. A multitude of ghosts flitted over these polished marble pavements and this happy sporting crowd welcoming new players to the coming basketball season. The shades of emperors and generals, slaves and gladiators, Christian missionaries and, much later, warriors hellbent on religious crusades. And teeming masses of ordinary men and women migrating to the richest city in the world to seek their fortune, people whose stories have never reached us even though their actions have shaped our future as much as the politicians and generals whose names we still remember.

By the time Rome took Brundisium she was propelled by her own momentum. The transition from city state to grasping, avaricious coloniser of other nations, all in less than a century, was never the intention of Appius. He was looking to win a local battle, to feed troops quickly and efficiently into the border dispute with a southern neighbour and ease the agonising shame of that defeat at the Caudine Forks. But that stirring speech he gave to the Senate not long before he died, urging them never to give up against Pyrrhus, marked the fact that this was a different, more ambitious city to the one in which he'd grown up. Now Italy was in Rome's grip his heirs were starting to peer acquisitively across the sea, wondering where to aim next.

It was inevitable such ambitions would never go unnoticed. On the other side of the Mediterranean another great nation was looking back.

❧ 6 ❧

HANNIBAL AT THE GATES

THE CITY that felt it had the most to lose from an acquisitive, militaristic Rome lay across the sea in North Africa: Carthage, today a suburb of Tunis, the capital of Tunisia. The two rivals had history already. Or to be more accurate, a genuine *storia*. Here we go back to that foundation-myth duly embroidered by Virgil, the poet who died where the Via Appia ended in Brundisium, stricken by an illness he caught sailing home after meeting the emperor Augustus, his patron, in Athens.

In his twelve-book poem the *Aeneid*, an ancient kind of *Game of Thrones* epic, Virgil recounts the story of the hero Aeneas from his flight after the Sack of Troy. It's stirring stuff in which, among other daring deeds, he defeats the man-eating cyclops Polyphemus then takes a trip into the underworld to meet his dead dad and see what happens to the wicked. In the final six books he arrives in Italy then, with a little help from his goddess mother, comes out top dog and marries the woman of his dreams. Only then does he sire the line that will one day produce Romulus, the founder of Rome, himself the father of the *gens Julia* which, combined with the *gens Claudia*, gave Rome its original line of emperors. Virgil was writing under the patronage of Augustus, the first of them, so he knew when flattery was needed. This was precisely what W. H. Auden was getting at when he wrote of him...

Behind your verse so masterfully made
We hear the weeping of a Muse betrayed.

The story of Aeneas wasn't the creation of Virgil. Various foundation-myths had been floating around long before his time, tales he managed to combine and embroider. One element he brought to the fore was the romance with an aristocrat named Dido after the Trojan hero washes up on the shore of North Africa.

Dido, queen of the newly founded city of Carthage.

It's an affair as doomed as it is briefly passionate. Dido listens to Aeneas's war stories and falls hopelessly in love. Here's the moment, in the seventeenth century translation by Britain's first poet laureate, John Dryden.

She fed within her veins a flame unseen;
The hero's valour, acts, and birth inspire
Her soul with love, and fan the secret fire.
His words, his looks, imprinted in her heart,
Improve the passion, and increase the smart.

Soon, while out hunting, the two of them enjoy the inevitable intimate encounter in a grove after which an ecstatic Dido believes she's as good as hitched. At this point, inevitably, the gods intervene the way gods do and remind Aeneas that duty always comes before love, and his destiny is to get back on his ships, sail to Italy and start a new nation there.

Dido throws one of the hissiest hissy fits in literature, shrieking her hatred for him, wishing him, his son and all his troops dead. Then she utters a terrifying curse. Dryden again...

Perpetual hate and mortal wars proclaim,
Against the prince, the people, and the name.
These grateful off'rings on my grave bestow;

> Nor league, nor love, the hostile nations know!
> Now, and from hence, in ev'ry future age,
> When rage excites your arms, and strength supplies
>   the rage
> Rise some avenger of our Libyan blood,
> With fire and sword pursue the perjur'd brood;
> Our arms, our seas, our shores, oppos'd to theirs;
> And the same hate descend on all our heirs!

In short, Dido is urging the Carthaginians who follow her to despise and pursue Aeneas and his offspring forever. After which she stabs herself and dies on her own funeral pyre. Quite an exit.

The Romans adored the *Aeneid* from the moment it appeared, posthumously and perhaps unrevised since Virgil was thought to be still working on it when he died close to those steps in Brundisium. In the Naples Archaeological Museum there's a touching fresco of Dido and Aeneas having a semi-naked snuggle that once adorned the walls of the so-called House of the Lyre Player in Pompeii. It was probably a popular painting in upper class bedrooms everywhere.

Two obvious references piqued the Roman imagination. The first was the idea of an upright hero being tempted from his true destiny by a sexy African queen. Virgil was writing shortly after the end of a real-life doomed tryst played out on an epic scale, that of Marc Antony and Cleopatra. They had committed suicide after Octavian, as Augustus was then known, defeated their forces and occupied the city of Alexandria. No Roman of Virgil's time would have missed the connection.

But there was another link too, Dido's warning that there would 'rise some avenger of our Libyan blood'.

ANYONE WHO HEARD that story at the time would know exactly who met the mythical queen's plea. He was born in Carthage in 247 BC as the Romans were engaged on a largely seaborne campaign against the city, the First Punic War – Punic means related to Carthage, a reference to the state's language, a version of Phoenician. It was a conflict that had begun seventeen years before, prompted by the hostile actions of one Appius Claudius Caudex, brother to the Appius Caecus who started this tale.

The boy was six when the war concluded in ignominy for the Carthaginians, with the loss of Sicily and the Aeolian Islands, Corsica and Sardinia, along with heavy financial penalties and ransoms for the return of their captured prisoners while Roman soldiers in custody returned home for nothing.

Three years later his father made the child dip his hand in blood and swear an oath of eternal hatred against Rome. He didn't hesitate for a moment. The lad came from a distinguished aristocratic family called Barca, which meant thunderbolt in Carthaginian. But everyone knew him as Hannibal.

When Hannibal said he hated the Romans, he meant it. And he had good reason. Carthage had been a great and cultured nation when sheep were still wandering through the Roman forum. Merchants by nature, the city traded the length of the Mediterranean, east and west, and beyond to Britain and the Atlantic coast of Africa. But the loss of Sicily and the Aeolian Islands to Rome was a political and economic setback that had left Carthage desperately worried its power and influence were on the wane. So, under the leadership of Hannibal's father, Hamilcar Barca, a Carthaginian force had begun to occupy Spain and build a new colony there. It was in Spain that the nine-year-old Hannibal was forced by his father to dip his hand in blood and swear eternal enmity to Rome. His home city across the sea was a place he'd see intermittently during his military and political career, and then mostly in defeat.

Hamilcar died subduing Spain for Carthage. Almost as soon as his successors began to establish mastery of Iberia, the Romans turned up, threatening trouble there too. While his brother Hasdrubal stayed in Spain to keep the locals in check and fight any Roman incursions, Hannibal set off on his celebrated trek through the Alps.

The idea of invasion, of foreigners seizing sovereign Italian territory, was repugnant to the Romans. Worse, Hannibal seemed better than they were at war, even when he was outnumbered. So terrifying did the spectre of this fearsome African general appear that for centuries afterwards Roman senators, fearful some disaster was approaching, would cry 'Hannibal ad portas!' Hannibal is at the gates. Yet he only approached the walls of Rome once then retreated even though his close friend Maharbal, second-in-command of the Carthaginian army, couldn't wait to attack. 'You, Hannibal, know how to gain a victory,' Maharbal told him. 'You do not know how to use it.'

The story of Hannibal's fifteen years roaming Italy with his forces, never managing to make Rome surrender, is one too long and complex to be told in detail here. But his extraordinary campaign deserves a place in any account of the Via Appia since it demonstrates how important control of the road had become. The Romans saw it as their means to take their army to the front. Now Hannibal turned the tables on them and monopolised Appius's highway for himself.

If he couldn't seize Rome he needed a base, somewhere central, with good transportation links. A permanent headquarters for a makeshift army composed of mercenaries from North Africa, slingshot warriors from the Balearics, elephant handlers and renegades from Latin tribes who'd come to his side. The place he picked was the same city Appius had decided was to be the hub for Rome's push against the Samnites. Today's modest town of Santa Maria Capua Vetere. Back then, the much wealthier and more independent-minded Capua.

ALOOF, suspicious of others, and quietly ambitious, the Capuans had always owned mixed feelings about the northerners who kept pushing them around from Rome. They welcomed the trade and the money the road had brought them. But, like most of the towns and cities up and down Italy, they were aware of being in thrall to others, not masters of their own destiny. Outsiders, not quite foreigners but lacking the status of full Roman citizenship. Provincials looked down on by the city slickers to whom they paid obeisance and constant taxes.

Hannibal had spies out in the field, testing the local temperature. Several Greek cities had switched sides already. So he found himself pushing at an open door when he approached the elders of Capua and asked if they wanted to strike a deal. In return for help he promised money, military support and independence. In a redrawing of the territorial lines of Italy, Capua, not Rome, would be the new capital of the south. It didn't take them long to agree.

Hannibal stationed his troops on the slopes of nearby Mount Tifata. The Capuans rubbed their hands and waited for the good times to begin. Tifata is still pretty much unchanged, a hilly, wooded wilderness perfect for a wandering army. Bordered to the north by the broad Volturno river with open plains on most sides, it was impossible for enemy troops to approach by stealth. An ideal defensive position to take. I drew a blank trying to find traces of Hannibal anywhere along the length of the Via Appia and elsewhere. He was a man for razing cities, not building them. The decade and a half the Carthaginian spent at war in Italy shaped Roman military and political thinking for centuries to come. Yet his legacy lies mostly in the pages of history books and on the walls of art galleries around the world. Like ancient Capua, now renamed and much reduced in importance, he was heading for a fall.

Maharbal's taunt – You know how to gain a victory, not how to use it – was part of the explanation. When there was a pitched battle Hannibal was in his element, and his tactics are still studied and taught in military establishments around the world. Taking and holding key cities were very different challenges. His targets were usually protected by thick, high walls, and troops trained to rain arrows, oil and fire on any who approached them. The easiest way to win them over was the method he used with Capua – bribes and offers of freedom from Rome. The hardest was brute force. Something Hannibal didn't fear, but he lacked the means. A siege required time, resources, equipment and specialist engineers he'd never managed to bring through the Alps. Resources that could only come by sea – and for all his efforts no great port in Italy had come to his side. He could command much of the Via Appia. But all he had was land, not reliable access to the Adriatic or the Tyrrhenian.

There was a third way, though. This was a general who late in life won a sea battle by the unique method of launching barrels of venomous snakes onto the decks of his enemies. Trickery was never far from his mind.

He needed a port, large, with excellent communications facilities. There was one obvious direction to look. South, along the Via Appia, to a city that, sixty years before, had fought and lost its own war against Rome. With luck and intrigue, Tarentum might be persuaded to change its allegiance again.

Capua could look after itself for a while.

ON A MARCH NIGHT in 212 BC, the Roman guards at the southern gates of Tarentum heard a familiar whistle outside their post. These soldiers were part of an unwelcome occupying force. The locals hated everything about them except their money, but for the military it was a cushy posting, with good food and wine and any entertainment they wanted in a place with a notorious reputation for decadence.

If they felt threatened, all they need do was retreat across the bridge from the residential area of the city, back to the little island of the Old Town where I'd parked my Abarth wondering whether it would still be there in the morning. Two and a bit millennia ago this wasn't the rundown, laundry-strewn straggle of homes and shops it is today. It was the Romans' fortress where, from behind its own high walls, they could control the outlet from the Mare Piccolo and all maritime traffic.

The Roman sentries had become used to that whistle beyond the wall that separated Tarentum from the flat open land where the Via Appia ran across to Brundisium. It belonged to a local called Philomenus, a young blade who'd taken to going out hunting in the countryside with his mates, coming back with game that often wound up on the tables of the Roman military.

Two years after arriving in Italy, Hannibal had wiped out the largest Roman army ever assembled at Cannae, north west of modern Bari, inflicting losses amounting to between seventy and eighty thousand killed or captured. By the usual rules of ancient warfare a defeat on this scale should have heralded the moment Rome threw in the towel and negotiated an embarrassing peace with the invaders from across the Mediterranean. But the Senate wasn't interested in the usual rules. The ancient warning of the Samnite elder Herennius stood as firm as ever: humiliate the Romans and they won't rest until they've made you pay for it many times over.

Desperate, divided, so short of money generals were raiding the revered temples for gold and silver and weapons, the Romans kept on going. At one point, following some religious guidance from the augurs, they'd even buried alive two men and two women, Gauls and Greeks, in the forum to appease the gods, an act of human sacrifice that was thought horrifying but necessary. On a more practical level its armies were developing different tactics to avoid another catastrophe like Cannae. Under new leadership, they refused to fight large-scale pitched battles. Hannibal excelled at those. Instead they harried him, nipping at his heels, choosing small skirmishes, not the mass encounters which had cost so much before.

Big fight or little one, Hannibal had proved himself a different kind of general, one who was never above deceit or tied to the military strategies of old. Philomenus, the hunter who'd been bringing the Romans good game for weeks, was key to one of his many ruses. Rome had always had doubts about Tarentum's loyalties so, in the fevered state of Italy, the city had seized hostages to ensure the Tarentines stayed on side as Hannibal waged his roving war. A handful of homesick prisoners had tricked their way out of captivity in Rome, only to be seized fleeing south along the Via Appia at Tarracina. They were returned, whipped in public, then thrown to their deaths from the Tarpeian Rock, the cliff on the Capitol where traitors traditionally met their grim fate.

Tarentum was unamused, Philomenus and his chums more than most. On the pretext of another hunting expedition, they snuck out of the walls and approached Hannibal, offering to help him win a way into the city. A deal was struck, a plan laid. Hannibal let it be known that he was sick and moved east with his forces to convince the Romans he was headed elsewhere. Then Philomenus and his peers began to make nightly excursions, always returning with game and stolen cattle to keep the Romans sweet – some provided by the Carthaginians themselves.

That March night the men outside the gates hadn't finished hunting. They were about to start. As a Roman sentry admired the gigantic boar the party returned with, Philomenus skewered him with his sword, and the rest of the party, Hannibal's men for the most part, began their attack. Soon the city gates were open and the Carthaginians began flooding through. It was dark and to begin with the Tarentines believed it was the Romans who were ransacking the city. Then with dawn they saw the bloodied corpses on the street and realised Tarentum was now under Carthaginian rule. Hannibal's orders had been plain: kill all Romans, leave the citizens untouched. That morning he had the locals assemble in the agora – the Greek word for forum was still in use – and issued an order for all local houses to have the word 'Tarentine' painted on their doors. Any without that were judged to be Roman and could be plundered at will.

Wandering around sleepy modern Taranto, it's hard to imagine the slaughter that must have happened that day. It looks much like any other ordinary southern city, a little worse for wear except around the gardens of the Piazza Garibaldi, a quiet, open space not far from the museum.

Across the swing bridge, there are still fortifications. The fifteenth-century Castello Aragonese there was built for the then King of Naples. It's a little like a larger and more fetching version of the fortress in Venosa, though this time there's sea lapping against the walls. It's now in the hands of the Italian navy who will happily escort visitors around for free. Excavations have shown that this was used as a fortress as far back as Greek times. When Hannibal snuck his murdering troops into the city across the narrow stretch of water by its side, much of the island of the Old Town was protected by fortress walls like these.

The Romans, civilians and soldiers, who managed to escape his murderous troops fled here, on foot, swimming and by boat, desperate to find protection from the bloodthirsty Carthaginians and Tarentines plundering, murdering and raping their way through the city proper.

As that grim day wore on it became clear only a narrow stretch of water and a circlet of stone walls stood between them and the bloody fate being meted out to their kin, men, women and children, across the way.

~

YET THE FINAL VICTORY, and the slaughter of every last Roman in Tarentum, never happened. If you walk round the perimeter of the Old Town today, dodging the traffic and the scaffolding, it's not hard to see why. Small it may be, but this is a real island perched in the middle of a channel leading from the Mare Piccolo to the sea beyond. Behind its impregnable walls the Romans found themselves safe, able to repel Hannibal's forces with ease.

After a while it became obvious they were, in some ways, faring better than the supposed victors of the city's capture. Roman forces still controlled the waterway in and out of the Mare Piccolo. This meant they could be resupplied with food and men from the sea and, at the same time, keep the Tarentine fleet trapped in the inner lagoon. Any vessel that tried to escape through the narrow canal to the ocean came under immediate and devastating attack. Ever innovative, Hannibal had some Tarentine ships dragged out of the inner harbour and hauled through the main town, then launched back into the water. But this was hard and awkward and still he didn't have what he needed: a port capable of handling the ships that would bring him money, heavy equipment and yet more skilled and experienced troops.

Two hundred miles north along the Via Appia, Capua was in trouble, besieged by Roman forces, starving, unable even to send out messengers until one finally slipped out at night and rode south to Hannibal asking for help. He agreed, gave up trying to force a way into the citadel of the Old Town and took his cavalry and foot soldiers north where they failed to break the Roman forces blockading the city he'd promised so much.

Then he rolled the dice again. Hannibal finally decided to march on the capital, believing the offensive would draw away the troops besieging Capua and allow it to be resupplied. The Romans weren't fooled. If he hadn't turned on Rome after the massive victory at

Cannae why would he try now? Livy reports that Hannibal's army went down the older, slower Via Latina. The Romans from Capua took the more direct Via Appia, stopping at all the towns and villages and warning them to take in crops and form brigades to guard their communities against the Carthaginians.

Hannibal stopped three miles short of Rome's walls and waited for battle... which, a few skirmishes apart, never came. The weather was grim, thunderstorms and torrential rain. Then a messenger came in and revealed the spot of land on which he'd fixed his camp had recently been sold at auction in Rome. The fact he was there and would surely claim it as the spoils of war in victory didn't even affect the price. Furious, Hannibal immediately announced he was going to sell all the silversmiths' shops in the Roman Forum when he captured the city. But the game was up. His ruse of drawing enemy troops away from Capua hadn't worked.

The city that had turned against Rome was lost, and its leaders knew it. Twenty seven of them laid on a grand banquet, got steaming drunk then took poison. The next day the city gates opened to the besieging forces. Another seventy or more who were judged to be part of Capua's defection to Hannibal were whipped then beheaded in public. Rome debated what to do with its treacherous southern neighbour. Economics saved Capua from total ruin: it was judged too rich and important an agricultural centre to be razed to the ground as some wanted. Instead, says Livy...

It was settled that Capua itself should be simply... a city merely in name; there was to be no corporate life, no senate, no council of the plebs, no magistrates; the population were without any right of public assembly or self-government; they had no common interest and were incapable of taking any common action. The administration of justice was in the hands of a praetor who was to be sent annually from Rome. In this way matters were arranged at Capua in pursuance of a policy which commends itself from every point of view. Sternly and swiftly was punishment meted out to those who had been most guilty, the civic population was scattered far and wide with no hope of return, the unoffending walls and houses were spared from the ravages of fire and demolition.

The surviving nobles were thrown into prison. The rest of the population were sold as slaves. Rome wanted everyone in Italy to understand what happened to those who betrayed its trust. They got the message too. Soon towns and cities everywhere that had sided, publicly or privately with Hannibal, made it clear they were with Rome after all.

Two years later the war was still in the balance when Hannibal suffered another painful blow. Tarentum, where he was still besieging the citadel without success, fell to Roman forces through precisely the same kind of trick he'd used to seize it in the first place. The city was put to the sword without mercy.

Six years on Hannibal's Italian adventure was over. He sailed for Carthage from Crotona (Crotone), the one port he'd managed to hold. Rome had learned the lessons he'd taught them. One of their own had taken the battle across the Mediterranean and struck at the heart of Carthage itself.

LET'S go back to Rome for a while because the next part of Hannibal's story most certainly began there, in the circles of an aristocratic family of some fame. Before the Via Appia reaches the Aurelian Wall it's known as the Via Porta San Sebastiano. The first stretch is broad, busy and unremarkable. But carry on and the old road begins to appear, narrow, with pretty geometric Sampietrini cobbles and high walls on both sides, thronged with busy traffic. On the left as you head out, shortly before the Porta San Sebastiano itself, there's a metal gate with a sign: *Sepolcro degli Scipioni*.

The burial place of one of Rome's most celebrated families sits in the *Parco degli Scipioni*, a delightful green oasis full of archaeological remains, broad avenues, gardens and exotic trees. Just outside the gate onto the Via di Porta Latina is a tiny circular church called *San Giovanni in Oleo* − literally 'St John in oil'. This is built on the spot where local legend has it the saint was boiled in oil by the emperor Domitian. When, miraculously, he survived unharmed, the watching crowd supposedly cried for his release. Domitian relented and sent him off to exile in Patmos where he wrote the Book of Revelation. One more saintly episode of legend running alongside the Via Appia.

There's an extensive columbarium – a repository for funerary urns that resembles a dovecote, hence the name – that belonged to a freed slave made good, Pomponius Hylas. But you can only see that by booking a group tour with the Rome archaeological administration. The same goes for the actual burial place of the Scipios too. So all the casual traveller can do is stare through the bars and use your imagination: it may look a little like an out-of-the-way entrance to the underworld now, but once this was a towering aristocratic tomb complex standing over the Via Appia, a monument to the greatness of the clan that built it. There so that travellers could marvel at their proximity to one of the most famous families Rome ever produced.

The Scipios furnished the city with at least fifteen consuls, some of whom served more than once. They were immensely wealthy, educated, ambitious, interested in fine living and, when the opportunity came along, the first to try to get to the front of any military action going.

Publius Cornelius Scipio had more than patriotic reasons to want to bring Hannibal to heel. He'd entered the wars at the age of eighteen, saving his father's life at one of the first battles against Hannibal in Italy, and managing to survive the catastrophe of Cannae too. In 211 BC, when he was twenty five, his father and his uncle both died fighting Hannibal's brother, Hasdrubal, in Spain. Scipio volunteered to replace them as commander of an army most regarded as a lost cause. In the space of five years he won the Spanish tribes to his side and defeated the Carthaginian forces outside modern-day Seville. Rome, under Scipio, was now fighting the kind of roaming, ruthless war that Hannibal had brought to Italy, and with rather more success.

It wasn't all one way. In 208 BC Hannibal staged that successful ambush we encountered earlier, killing the 'Sword of Rome', Marcus Claudius Marcellus, outside Venusia, leaving behind that sad little relic of a tomb, stones held together by cement down a back street of the modern town. But increasingly he was on the back foot, getting pushed further south into Bruttium (Calabria). To make matters worse, his brother, Hasdrubal, died in a savage defeat in the north. The

Romans cut off his head and threw it in a sack into Hannibal's Calabrian camp.

After his success in Spain, Scipio sailed for North Africa and found himself allies, which was why Carthage, in desperation, finally summoned Hannibal back across the Mediterranean. In 202 BC the two sides met outside Carthage in the Battle of Zama. By now the Romans had tactics to deal with Hannibal's war elephants. They frightened them with trumpets, let the lumbering beasts through their lines, attacked them in the rear with such ferocity they even managed to turn some of the terrified animals back on their own side. The battle was lost with as many as twenty thousand Carthaginian dead, and the same number captured. With it ended the Second Punic War.

CARTHAGE WAS LEFT bankrupt and constrained by such punishing capitulation terms it could never hope to recover. Scipio, for his success, was dubbed Scipio Africanus and returned a hero, though one envied and even hated by some of his political rivals back in Rome. Hannibal served as a politician in Carthage for a while but eventually fled, knowing he was on Rome's wanted list, fearing someone would betray him before long.

There followed an extended, itinerant exile in which he was hunted constantly, much as the Americans searched for Osama Bin Laden after the atrocities of 9/11. Finally, twenty or so years after Zama – the exact date is disputed – he was cornered in distant Bithynia, modern Anatolia in Turkey. As the Roman troops approached, determined they wouldn't be allowed to murder him on the spot or, worse, drag him back to Rome for humiliation and execution, he took poison. Supposedly before he died he said, 'Let us now relieve the Romans of their fears by the death of a feeble old man.'

By the time he killed himself those cities and towns he'd once won to his side along the Via Appia and elsewhere in Italy were firmly in Rome's grasp. Scipio Africanus died around the same time, in a kind of exile too. Political machinations at Rome had sickened him so much he'd retired to his farm in Liternum in Campania, close to the sea north of Neapolis. There, ill and bitter at his treatment at the hands of a hostile Roman Senate, he lived in modest circumstances, farming the fields himself at times.

On his deathbed he left orders that he should be buried on the farm, beneath the inscription, 'Ungrateful fatherland, you will not even have my bones'. So that capacious family tomb by the busy urban stretch of the Via Appia, seen by most of us through locked iron gates, never contained the ashes of the most famous Scipio of all.

AROUND THIRTY FIVE years after Hannibal's suicide, Rome engineered a final war with Carthage, one led by the adopted grandson of Africanus, Scipio Aemilianus, or Scipio Africanus the Younger. It was a short affair, one Carthage tried desperately to avoid, but Rome had no interest in peace. When the city finally fell it was razed on the orders of the Senate, against Scipio's wishes. The city burned for seventeen days and as many as a hundred and fifty thousand Carthaginians died.

The historian Polybius, Scipio's tutor from when he was young, accompanied the campaign and witnessed how the city was stormed. His account is lost but a later writer, Appian, must have seen it. He wrote...

> *Scipio, when he looked upon the city as it was utterly perishing and in the last throes of its complete destruction, is said to have shed tears and wept openly for his enemies. After being wrapped in thought for long, and realising that all cities, nations, and authorities must, like men, meet their doom; that this happened to Ilium, once a prosperous city, to the empires of Assyria, Media, and Persia, the greatest of their time, and to Macedonia itself, the brilliance of which was so recent, either deliberately or the verses escaping him, he said:*
>
> > *A day will come when sacred Troy shall perish,*
> > *And Priam and his people shall be slain.*
>
> *And when Polybius speaking with freedom to him, for he was his teacher, asked him what he meant by the words, they say that without any attempt at concealment he named his own country, for which he feared when he reflected on the fate of all things human.*

Like his grandfather before him, Scipio Aemilianus fell foul of Roman politics and died, possibly murdered, at odds with many of those in the Senate. Perhaps they didn't like his gloomy use of a quotation from Homer's *Iliad* about the sack of Troy and the thought that, one day, a rich and prosperous Rome might perish like the Carthage he'd seen destroyed in front of his eyes.

7

A DICTATOR IN THE WINGS

TERRACINA IS A HANDSOME SEASIDE TOWN, an ideal weekend break for Romans looking to escape the city. When it was ancient Tarracina the place was much the same, though the road journey through the malarial marshes was one of the most hated sections of the entire Via Appia. To make it easier for those who could afford it, eager Roman engineers dug a nineteen-mile canal, the Decennovium, for the last stretch to the coast. It's still there, next to the busy road, though only thanks to a reconstruction by an eighteenth century Pope. Winding past farm fields and grazing buffalo, it was much the faster way to get through the mosquito-ridden marshes. Not that our poet friend Horace was much impressed.

On his journey to Brundisium he recounts that by the time he'd left Aricia for Tarracina he was already 'at war with his belly'. Then came the night on the marsh.

The cursed gnats and frogs of the fens make sleep impossible while the boatman and a passenger, well-soaked with plenty of thick wine, try to outdo each other singing the praises of their absent lovers. Finally the passenger, tired out, begins to sleep and the lazy waterman ties the halter of the mule to a stone and lets it feed then snores away, lying flat on his back. And now the day arrives and still the boat's going nowhere. Until, that is, a furious fellow, one of the passengers, leaps out of the boat, and whacks the head and sides of both mule and boatman with a willow cudgel. Even by the middle of the morning, we're still not there.

There are still a few bugs around, but not as many as there used to be, and malaria's long gone. From Terracina beach you get a wonderful view back to the Temple of Jupiter Anxur on the hill that leads to Sperlonga.

The follower of the Via Appia can walk a genuine urban piece of it here. A photogenic, well-polished stretch served as ancient Tarracina's *decumanus*, its High Street, and still leads directly into what was once the ancient forum, now the Piazza del Municipio. It's a pretty, pedestrianised spot, with restaurants, shops and cafes, a small civic museum too. Around the quiet square through which the Via Appia now passes there are remains of temples, houses, a triumphal arch and the ruins of tombs nearby. The position, on top of a low hill, made military sense, and the harbour proved a busy port. Rome had taken control of the town early in its territorial adventures, in 315 BC and poured money and resources into it over the centuries.

Tarracina was lucky. A map of Italy in 100 BC tells a very interesting story. The country as a whole is under Roman control, but not in a uniform way. Many places fortunate enough to be situated along the busy Via Appia were now either direct Roman territory or colonies, the people there Roman citizens with all the rights that followed. The rest of the country was divided between Rome's Latin allies, who were denied full citizenship but held some preferential rights, and the rest, known as the *socii*, who, while still born and raised in Italy, got the roughest deal of all. They had to pay taxes, perform military service when required, but had none of the benefits of citizenship. As for foreigners, if they didn't have a Roman or Greek background there was a word for them: barbarians. Primitives, uneducated, backward.

The way key cities had so swiftly changed sides and backed Hannibal surely demonstrated their allegiance could never be taken for granted. Rome's response to disloyalty was always the one it had delivered to both defeated Capua and Carthage: more force, more cruelty, more death and slavery. Fifteen hundred years on another Italian, Niccolò Machiavelli, mused, 'One ought to be both feared and loved, but as it is difficult for the two to go together, it is much safer to be feared than loved, if one of the two has to be wanting.'

Rome didn't need any lessons on that front. Fear was the weapon they used everywhere, at home but especially abroad. A few of them understood this already and were beginning to be appalled by the cruelty the city's rulers displayed towards those it defeated. The younger Scipio's gloomy comments after the razing of Carthage showed that the policy of shock and awe demanded by the Senate was an order he felt bound to follow, but not one he agreed with.

The historian Tacitus, writing about a Roman campaign in Scotland, reports a speech by a native chieftain, Calgacus, in which he castigates his enemy's brutality and avarice.

Robbers of the world, having by their universal plunder exhausted the land, they rifle the deep. If the enemy are rich, they are rapacious; if he's poor, they lust for control; neither the east nor the west has been able to satisfy them. Alone among men they covet with equal eagerness poverty and riches. To robbery, slaughter, plunder, they give the lying name of empire; they make a desert and call it peace.

This was probably invention on the historian's part. There was, in all likelihood, no Calgacus, no speech at all. Tacitus, a senator from a wealthy Roman family, was delivering harsh judgement on his peers.

Rome had no desire to be loved. Fear was all it took. For the wealthy merchants of Tarracina and their visitors from the city, life was sweet beside the clear blue waters of the Tyrrhenian Sea. Elsewhere the same kind of resentment that had led cities like Capua to abandon Rome for a foreign power still festered.

IT WASN'T JUST about being the underdogs. There was also the pressing question of land. The wars and the expansion of Rome had changed how people lived in ways no one expected, and some had yet to understand. Drive from Terracina to Benevento today and you'll hardly see a square foot of open ground that doesn't grow something for the table or bottle or provide rich pasture for livestock. Some of the finest mozzarella in the world – from buffalo, naturally, not cows – comes from round here. The soil is rich and any Campanian will tell you there's nothing like a tomato grown in volcanic earth.

Before the Romans went walkabout, the fields of tribes like the Samnites were used by itinerant communities and shepherds or home to peasant farmers selling what they could and living off the rest. It was the kind of pastoral scene portrayed as idyllic by writers like Virgil, dreaming of a time when Italy was pure and innocent, untainted by bloodshed and war. The reality was more like poverty and subsistence agriculture, but Romans were as prone to falling for myths about the good old days as anyone else. The last thing the rich patrons of Virgil adoring his poetry would have wanted was to work the hard fields of Campania.

In any case, ownership of that idyllic landscape of Virgil had altered greatly as Rome grew. War needed soldiers, men often conscripted from rural communities, seized along the road. While they fought and died in the Senate's battles, the politicians back home grew fat and ever more wealthy on the booty, indemnities and commercial opportunities those conflicts brought. More and more any Roman nobleman of note needed a string of country properties to demonstrate his position in society, all bought with the new-found wealth that came with conquest. A mansion or two in Rome wasn't enough. They craved villas by the coast and rural estates, easily reachable along the fast roads spreading out from the capital. Country piles with land, naturally, as much as could be had, often for a pittance.

Just as modern agriculture has replaced small family farms with vast agribusinesses, the gentry of Rome made the humble smallholder uneconomic and kicked him off his fields. The poor flocked to the cities to try to make a living. The rich filled their new country holdings, known as *latifundia*, with slaves and found themselves making even more money than before. Soldiers, meanwhile, badgered the politicians who'd sent them to war for the promised patch of land on their return – and a barren field of rocks in one of those distant lands they'd just conquered was rarely going to satisfy them. They wanted somewhere near home, in Italy. The peasant farmers were trapped from both directions.

The question of land reform was taken up by an aristocrat called Tiberius Gracchus, grandson of Scipio Africanus. 'The wild beasts that roam over Italy have their dens, each has a place of repose and refuge. But the men who fight and die for Italy enjoy nothing but the air and light; without house or home they wander about with their wives and children,' he said, proposing in 134 BC a law that would distribute land to the poor and the homeless.

He was beaten to death by furious senators, along with three hundred of his supporters, while others who'd backed him were sewn into sacks with vipers. Ten years later his younger brother Gaius took up the same land reform cause to the fury of the Senate and was soon murdered by his opponents in a bloody confrontation, along with large numbers of his followers.

The anger reform provoked in political circles eventually led to the formation of two factions in the faltering republic. The *Optimates* (the best ones) were conservative, against change, on the side of the old patrician families against the emerging middle classes. Right wing we might call them in today's parlance. The *Populares* were, as the name suggests, claiming to be on the side of the people as a whole, keen on reform and extending Roman citizenship to allies. More centrist than left wing if you want to stick a modern tag on them, since a few of the aristocracy signed up to the club, among them Julius Caesar and Appius Claudius Pulcher, a descendant of our old road-building friend.

Wealth and property only stoked divisions in the Senate and the chattering upper classes. It wasn't long before that local bickering in Rome would explode into one more war.

TRAVELLING around the Benevento region you'll find the word 'Irpini' on streets, on businesses, the menus of restaurants for the occasional local dish, and Irpinia is a local wine region that's been lauded by some as the new Tuscany. The word comes from 'Hirpini', the tribe who'd left their home in Benevento in 321 BC to join their fellow Samnites defeating the Romans at the Caudine Forks. They'd sided with Hannibal for a while too, still harbouring a grudge against their masters up the road. In 90 BC they were up in arms against the Romans once more, this time along with pretty much all of Italy that didn't have the benefit of citizenship or the advantage of being Latin.

On the coast, Herculaneum (Ercolano) and Pompeii had both rebelled and were soon under siege. So too was another key Hirpini stronghold, Aeclanum, fifteen miles south east of Benevento. Today Pompeii and Herculaneum are packed with tourists lured by the story of two towns and their people smothered in volcanic dust and lava when Vesuvius erupted nearly two centuries later. Sights worth seeing undoubtedly, despite the crowds, though many of the treasures uncovered there now sit elsewhere, mostly in the archaeological museum of Naples.

Aeclanum, sixty miles west of Vesuvius, escaped the violent eruption but was very much a part of the rebellion known as the Social War – from the term *socii* – that gripped Italy for three years from 90 BC. It's easily missed as you drive past the place today, with nothing more than a small sign by the road outside the agricultural village of Passo di Mirabella. Down a dusty lane lie the remains of one of the most important settlements of the Hirpini, and the scene of a victory by a Roman general who was going to reshape the republic for good.

His full name was Lucius Cornelius Sulla Felix, though everyone knew him as Sulla. 'Felix' can mean 'happy' or just 'fortunate'. Sulla is one of the most bloodthirsty and ruthless figures to appear in Roman politics to date – which is saying something. Fortunate he might have been in his battles and political wiles over the years. Happy is pushing it for a man who wrote the motto for his own tomb, 'No friend ever served me, and no enemy ever wronged me, whom I have not repaid in full.'

After sacking Pompeii and Herculaneum, leaving them in no doubt what happens when you mess with Rome, Sulla turned his attention to Aeclanum and demanded its surrender. The town asked for a little while to consider its options. Sulla gave them an hour and set his soldiers placing faggots around the wooden barricade that guarded the place. When the hour was up, he set fire to the walls. The locals surrendered and then found themselves plundered in any case since Sulla resented the fact he'd had to burn them out. The scale of the settlement he took is just about visible with baths, temples, forum, houses, the remains of a theatre and a *macellum*, a covered market where meat and vegetables were sold, all set around the Via Appia.

The Social War proved short and bloody, with a death toll running as high as three hundred thousand. For once it concluded in the victorious Romans making an important compromise. Most of those who'd taken up arms against Rome, at one point aiming to set up a rival nation with a capital named Italica near Corfinio in Abruzzo, were given full citizenship. There wasn't the slightest generosity in this; Rome needed men to fight other wars abroad and was struggling to find them. And the offer only extended to those who agreed to lay down their weapons. Anyone thinking of taking up arms against Rome once more was left in no doubt about the consequences.

Sulla, however, was one of the Optimates, the conservative class, wary of all reform. He wasn't done.

One year later his troops were still besieging the last major city of the Hirpini to hold out against Rome, Nola. This was a place as stubborn as it was rich, twenty miles south east of Capua along one of Rome's new, fast feeder roads into the Via Appia, the Via Popilia which ran for more than three hundred and twenty miles to the toe of Italy at Rhegium (Reggio di Calabria) opposite Sicily on the Strait of Messina. Their boss was in the capital, newly elected consul, looking forward to sailing his army across the Adriatic for a war with a recalcitrant king called Mithridates in Pontus, modern Anatolia.

Then he found himself well and truly stiffed behind his back, and fearing for his life. His political opponents passed a law stripping him of command of the army, gave it to an arch rival, and dispatched messengers to the troops at Nola telling them they had a new commander. Sulla fled Rome as his supporters were attacked and killed in the street. When he returned to Nola, his men turned on the envoys who'd tried to impose upon them a different general, and, with their old boss at their head, did the unthinkable: they trooped north to Rome, took the city, burned houses, slaughtered locals who opposed them, and placed him back in charge.

No one had ever entered Rome like this before. It was sacrilege to cross the city boundaries in arms. But Sulla, like so many despots before and after, told everyone he was freeing the city from tyrants. This bloody, enforced peace didn't last. Sulla was impelled to take his army to Greece and Pontus to fight the ambitious Mithridates. As soon as he was abroad his enemies were back, murdering his allies in Rome by the hundreds, seizing power once more, sentencing Sulla to death *in absentia*.

In the spring of 83 BC Sulla sailed from Patras in Greece to Brundisium with a formidable army of forty thousand men, a navy of sixteen hundred ships and untold gold and silver from all the cities he'd plundered in the east. The port knew which side its bread was buttered and welcomed him with open arms, so much that he spared them any taxes. A full-scale civil war was now under way between the Senate and its renegade former consul. On the first of November 82 BC, after a decisive battle outside the city walls at the Colline Gate, Rome belonged to Sulla once more. He was about to set the tone for the final two years of his political life.

Across the road from the Capitol Hill, close to the Roman ghetto, stands the circular Teatro Marcello, a first century BC auditorium reminiscent of the Colosseum in some ways though in rather finer nick. Above the original arches of the ground floor sits the Palazzo Orsini, one of the swishest and most expensive addresses in town. I used to dream about living there while I was writing books set in Rome. Though given the last time it went on the market, in 2012, the asking price was a mere $26 million I'd definitely need to shift a few more copies. By the side of the theatre, along from the ghetto and its excellent Jewish restaurants, sits a jumble of ruins, all that's left of the Temple of Bellona, built by the busy Appius Claudius

Caecus to give thanks for his victories against the Samnites and the Etruscans.

After his triumph at the Colline Gate, Sulla summoned the terrified senators here. Since the temple was devoted to a goddess associated with the fury of war, they must have gone along wondering if they'd ever return to their families. As he began to talk terrified shrieks rang out from a neighbouring public building. They were the death cries of between six and eight thousand prisoners captured after the battle, all of whom had surrendered on the promise of being spared. Now they were being butchered one by one. Sulla was making his point: obey me or die. And many were to perish, whether they obeyed him or not.

Ask most people who they think of as Rome's first dictator and the chances are they'll name Julius Caesar or Augustus. No, it was Lucius Cornelius Sulla Felix. Shortly after capturing Rome he made the Senate give him that title and absolute power over most of the empire except Hispania. Ever since they threw out their last king more than four centuries before, the city's political structure had been based on the idea that no man could exercise sole control of Rome, only two consuls elected annually.

During the dark days of the war against Hannibal that had been relaxed out of military need, but only for six months. Now Sulla seized it for himself without time limit and embarked upon a savage campaign of reprisals against anyone he deemed an enemy, one quite unlike the frequent, spontaneous violent outbursts of before. He initiated an idea later emperors were to grow to love: a list of proscriptions, the names of men he regarded as enemies of the state, marking them down for execution and the seizure of all their properties. Those who killed someone on the proscribed list were awarded money. Anyone who hid them was marked down for death as well. As many as nine thousand citizens are thought to have perished, sometimes for very little at all.

Sulla brought Rome two terrors the city would meet many times over the centuries to come. Not just proscriptions but the idea that one man, not two consuls, might wield absolute power, and for life, not just for a year. Four young shakers and movers on the political scene in particular, all destined for future fame and notoriety, were watching and taking note.

Marcus Licinius Crassus had commanded part of Sulla's army at the Colline Gate and become immensely rich in part from helping himself to the proceeds from the seized property of the victims of the proscriptions.

Gnaeus Pompey Magnus, the self-styled Pompey the Great, had scourged the remaining enemies of Sulla in Sicily and North Africa, and married Sulla's step-daughter.

Gaius Julius Caesar was wise enough to watch developments from distant Bithynia until Sulla's death since his uncle, Gaius Marius, was Sulla's greatest enemy which could easily have led to Caesar's name appearing on the proscription list.

And Marcus Tullius Cicero, an ambitious lawyer and writer with high political ambitions who had accompanied Sulla's army on his latest campaigns, though Cicero never saw himself as a military man and seems to have stayed away from the fighting, as he would throughout his life.

All of them saw opportunity beckoning as they watched Sulla rewrite the rules of Roman politics. All of them would die violently in the bloody years to come.

But not Sulla. At the end of 81 BC he shocked the city by standing down as dictator. The following year he spent as consul. Then he resigned all public office and wandered the Forum offering to explain his actions to any citizen who cared to listen. After that he retired to his villa in Puteoli outside Naples and set his mind on what he enjoyed most: eating and drinking and the company of sexual partners who included a female impersonator Sulla said he adored. While writing his memoirs, sadly lost, he became ill, gruesomely so if a few of the stories are to be believed, and died in 78 BC at the age of sixty.

According to Appian, Sulla's body was carried from the coast of Campania to Rome on a golden litter, trumpeters and horsemen riding in advance, soldiers flocking from all directions to join the procession. When the bier reached the city it was borne through the streets in an enormous parade, accompanied by golden crowns and other gifts. Then, in the Campus Martius, close to where he'd had those captives slaughtered within earshot of the terrified senators four years before, his funeral pyre was lit.

Some objected to all the pomp and pageantry for a man who'd spilled so much Roman blood. But mostly they felt it wise to stay silent. Sulla had given Rome its first taste of savage dictatorship. Yet, unlike any to follow in his footsteps, he'd willingly given up the throne to drink and write and cavort with his lovers by the seaside in Campania. Was he trying to teach Rome a lesson... that this was where softness and liberalism would lead? And that to maintain the strength and purpose of the republic it needed to knuckle down, take hard decisions, listen to older men, not the eager, fame-grabbing young? The complex reforms he'd made to the workings of the city's political structure certainly suggest this, since they bent the rules in favour of senior conservatives and against the younger Populares.

Or perhaps he simply felt he'd achieved everything he wanted and, after a long hard life, it was time for some riotous entertainment. It hardly mattered. Within a decade Sulla's changes to the constitution were undone, to a large extent by his protégé Pompey. His strange career would principally be remembered as a lesson in force and might. The revelation that any man with an army strong enough and the resources to support himself could turn centuries of tradition upside down and take war straight to the heart of Rome.

Pompey, Crassus and Caesar would have to wait to put that to the test. Five years after Sulla's spectacular funeral the city was once more looking down the Via Appia at Capua in astonishment.

Another war was looming, this time with creatures so lowly the offended senators could hardly believe their ears.

Their leader was a slave, scarcely human. A gladiator called Spartacus.

8

THE SLAVES STRIKE BACK

DRIVING INTO CAPUA – sorry, Santa Maria Capua Vetere – the place appeared so ordinary and provincial I wondered if the satnav was playing games. It seems like any other road town in Campania, a bit scruffy with some ragtag ribbon development, a fair bit quite ugly. Nearby is the busy E45 highway, itself a marvel of road-building, Europe's longest road, running, with a few gaps for sea, from Gela in Sicily, through Austria, Germany, Denmark, Sweden and Finland to Alta in the far north of Norway. More than three thousand miles crossing seven different countries. Appius would have been impressed.

My destination didn't feel international at all. There's scarcely a conventional hotel in town. Most people stay up the road in the provincial capital Caserta to visit Italy's equivalent of Versailles, the extremely grand eighteenth century royal palace built for the House of Bourbon. But Caserta didn't even exist when the Romans ruled the roost so, travelling blind as I often was off the beaten track, I booked a room over the internet and hoped for the best. This time I struck lucky. The 'room' turned out to be a large one-bedroomed apartment, half a divided house maintained by the friendly Pasquale. After more tortuous parking escapades than I could remember, Taranto being the worst, I found I could drive the Abarth straight up to the front door and leave her there for free. Which was all the more remarkable because Pasquale's room was right beside the most important historical artefact in town: the amphitheatre and the remains of the adjoining gladiator school which was supposedly the finest in Italy. Breakfast on my patio gave me a close-up view of the historic area where the next part of this story, the slave and peasant revolt begun by Spartacus, erupted.

A confession: I can't count how many times I've visited Rome, how many months I've spent there writing stories set in such an amazing city. Not once in all that time have I set foot in the Colosseum. There are so many delightful and interesting places to see that the idea of queuing for ages while being pestered by fake centurions with plastic swords has never appealed. If you really want to see a Roman amphitheatre, ancient Capua is the place. On the Saturday I turned up it was pretty much empty apart from a busy crowd of diners enjoying the excellent bar-restaurant set in its midst serving organic meat and vegetables from Campanian farms. The amphitheatre of old Capua was the second largest in Italy, just a touch smaller than the Colosseum, and that afternoon three of us had the whole place to ourselves. But not at night. There was a concert and two thousand years on Capua's amphitheatre was back doing what it was built for: entertaining the public.

No bloody fights to the death between gladiators and a few wild beasts from time to time. Just a local band and lots of people enjoying a balmy late summer evening. It's easy to warm to Santa Maria Capua Vetere, humble as it is compared to the place Cicero called 'Altera Roma', the second Rome. The amphitheatre we see today would never be recognised by Capua's most famous rebel, Spartacus. It was built around the start of the second century AD by which time he was another bloody part of history. When the uprising he led began, Capua had a smaller arena on this same spot.

The ruins, with their mosaics and a small rather theatrical gladiator museum, are all that remain of a complex of buildings that carried a kind of Las Vegas-style pomp about them. In the Naples Archaeological Museum you can find the 'Venus of Capua', a glamorous statue of the half-naked goddess that dates back to Hadrian's time and is stylisti-

cally related to the more famous Venus de Milo. With her dress tanta-
lisingly tumbling from her thighs, the goddess of love would have
pulled in plenty of crowds back when the place was in its prime.

Quite a show it must have been too. Sailors would have operated
the *velarium*, a vast sail-like awning drawn over the crowd to save them
from the sun and rain and stir a breeze through the galleries of the
arena. Around the arches statues of Roman gods would have looked
down on the spectators, along with theatrical masks, busts of Pan and
leering satyrs. In the centre of the arena, the wooden planked floor was
sprinkled with sand to soak up the inevitable gore. Beneath, visible
still, were the cells where gladiators, prisoners and wild animals would
await their fate. With a handful of visitors wandering around the stone
skeleton of the amphitheatre today, and people tucking in happily to
their organic lunches just a few steps away from the place where men,
and women, died repeatedly over the centuries, it's hard to imagine
what the atmosphere must have been like on fight day in ancient
Capua.

Excited. Full of anticipation. Wondering how many of the fallen
men in the arena that day would merit the down-turned thumbs of the
crowd that spelled death.

CAPUA'S GLADIATORS were confined to quarters close to the arena and
trained in public as part of the spectacle, just as they did in Rome at
the Ludus Magnus, the training facility close to the Colosseum, now an
archaeological site just across the road from the arena. In many ways
they were not unlike modern sporting heroes. They had their fan clubs
as ancient wall graffiti lauding individual fighters demonstrates. They
could keep the prizes they won, and enjoy female visitors – sometimes
upper-class women looking for a bit of a thrill – when they felt like it.
A famous gladiator could pull in crowds from miles around, making
lots of money for his master.

But he was still a prisoner, travelling from fight to fight in chains.
Slavery was one more by-product of the growth in international trade
that the new world of fast, easy transport had created. Shipped

through ports like Brundisium, Neapolis and Ostia, caged and manacled as they were carted along the road, they arrived in their thousands from all over the conquered world. Then would come the humiliation of the market where they'd be bought and sold like animals, judged on their strength, their age, their health, their beauty too.

The lucky ones – if you can call it that – were the educated, often Greeks, whose skills in medicine, learning and philosophy might win them places in the leading households of the day. There they could live comfortably, better than some of the more humble Roman citizens at times, and hope to win their precious freedom if they proved useful enough, or their masters, in their wills, felt sufficiently generous.

The illiterate who'd only worked fields would find themselves bought as cheap labour for the gigantic farms created by *latifundia*, often leading miserable lives of hard toil until, too old to be of any use, they were thrown out onto the street.

Then there were the fit, the strong, the former soldiers, battle-hardened, violent. Spartacus was just such a man. He came from Thrace, one more region where the Romans had effective control through a client king. What led Spartacus into slavery we don't know – some accounts say he fought the Romans and was captured. From what ensued it seems clear he had some military knowledge of how Roman armies fought, and would soon get the chance to use it.

Samnites, Etruscans, compliant Gauls, from north to south Italy was now, after the end of the Social War, full of Roman citizens. Perhaps the senators behind this, some of them with great reluctance, thought Italy was truly Roman throughout. They ignored the fact that the expansion of empire had brought slaves, almost all foreign, flooding into the country. By 73 BC there were probably a million or more, some treated well, others abominably. But, comfortable or not, they were all slaves, and many surely resented that every day they spent in servitude.

Sicily had already seen two slave rebellions. In the last, a thousand captured rebels had been ordered to the arena in Rome to die fighting wild animals. Instead, determined to resist the Romans to the last, they killed one another in turn, without a fight, until the last man used his blade upon himself. Slaves turning on their masters was not uncommon. As always, defiance was met with ruthless cruelty. If one slave rose and killed his or her master, every one of their fellow prisoners in the household – guilty or not – would be put to the sword.

There were at least twenty five different kinds of gladiator entertaining the crowds in the arenas. Spartacus was a famed 'murmillo', which meant he must have been a big fellow, broad in the shoulders, with muscular arms. The way he fought was always the same – barechested behind a large shield, with a short gladius sword and round his waist a decorated leather belt, much like the kind seen on modern boxers. His helmet would have borne a fish emblem while his sword arm would have been enclosed in some kind of metal guard. It's safe to say that, while later accounts would attest to his sense of equality and decency on occasion, he wasn't the sort of fellow you'd want to meet on a dark and lonely night.

Like his peers he was the property of the man who'd bought him and installed him in the gladiator school close to where happy diners now watch their kids play gladiator games with plastic swords and shields on the lawn. Lentulus Batiatus was a *lanista*, a businessman who bought, trained, and sold men for combat, and dispatched them to fights around Italy for a fee. We know very little about Batiatus. Some accounts claim he was a cruel master, so harsh that his slaves rose against him. Or perhaps Spartacus and his peers simply wanted to be free, to escape the bloody life of the arena. Either way about seventy gladiators broke out of the *ludus* owned by Batiatus, seized knives from the kitchen, and set out into an astonished Capua. There they stole better weapons from anyone they met, then set off into the countryside, taking what they could – money, clothes, food – from any they met.

Spartacus's name has come to be associated with freedom fighters everywhere. From operas to video games, TV series to countless novels, he's stood as a symbol of defiance against tyranny, most famously in Stanley Kubrick's film where Kirk Douglas's insistent 'I'm Spartacus' is taken up by all the defeated rebels around him. All good stories. And that's mostly what they are.

Still, he touched a chord in the people of Italy, and not just among gladiators and slaves. Hannibal had an army of skilled mercenaries, trained killers. He used the Via Appia and the roads that sprang from it to roam the length of the country seeking pitched battles that would force Rome to capitulate. Spartacus was enough of a military man to understand this would be his undoing. Roman forces lined the consular roads, organised and well-provisioned. The last thing a bunch of runaway slaves and outlaws needed was a pitched battle on the terms of a highly experienced general.

So from Capua his band of gladiators headed west towards the coast and the wild countryside on the green and open slopes of a Vesuvius a century away from the famous eruption that would swamp Pompeii and Herculaneum, towns then recovering from the punishments they'd received for rebelling during the Social War.

Rome, blind to what was happening, regarded these local events with disdain and disgust. These people were slaves. It wasn't a genuine war at all, just a little local rebellion caused by the scum of the earth who'd soon be dead or dangling from a cross. True military conflict involved high-born generals leading trained troops into the kind of formal engagement both sides understood. Not untrained civilians with home-made weapons and armour pretending they could take on the legions of Rome.

Besides, Roman forces were busy fighting wars, *real* wars abroad. In Spain Pompey was battling a turncoat Roman general. To the east, the fight against the dogged Mithridates continued in Greece and beyond. The last thing the Senate was going to be rattled by was a bunch of slaves and renegade layabouts wandering Campania robbing everyone they met. They were outlaws, desperadoes, criminals, not warriors.

A lot of outlaws very soon.

ITALY'S most famous peak looked very different back then. It was still a mountain, snow-topped in winter as it is, with its volcanic rim, today. But modern Vesuvius is hemmed on its sea side by Naples and the busy agricultural, industrial and tourist towns running along the shoreline towards Sorrento. I've spent a fair bit of time around there and can confirm a few are as rough and crime-ridden as anything Romans of two millennia ago would have known.

Away from the coast, though, the peak must be much as it was, verdant, bountiful, full of farms that could be plundered for food, horses and fresh recruits. Capua enjoyed its meat and vegetables just as much then as it does now – you only have to look at the menu from that restaurant by the arena to see that. So as word of Spartacus's successes spread, the outrage of its citizens grew at the idea a band of gladiators – slaves, no less – were taking liberties with the horn of plenty on its doorstep. A group of mercenaries set out from Capua spoiling for a fight, perhaps funded in part by the furious slave master Lentulus Batiatus. They were soon dealt with, robbed and slaughtered like the vanquished in the arena. Then the renegade band could throw away their own makeshift, sometimes home-made weapons and use ones of genuine military quality.

Word of the revolt was soon spreading through the countryside. Slaves began running away from their farms to join the camp on Vesuvius in search of freedom. The poor, the hungry, and the dispossessed were soon joining them, men, women, families too. Spartacus was ruthless with his enemies, but endeavoured to be fair to his new followers. They were treated with a respect they never received from their masters. Plunder was shared equally. Still, this was very much not an army and a former military man like Spartacus surely knew it. His camp was composed of people from many varied backgrounds and cultures, Gauls and Thracians, displaced Samnites, runaway Roman soldiers. They spoke different languages, followed different gods. While most regarded Spartacus as their leader, there were others with important positions too, and fierce tactical disagreements as time went on.

Finally, a force arrived from Rome to fight them. It was small, ill-trained, more a riot squad militia than a small army ready to fight a war. Spartacus resorted to the guerrilla tactics he would adopt until the very end. Avoid pitched battles, always use cunning. His men clambered down Vesuvius on what the Romans thought was an impossibly steep incline – supposedly using ropes made out of vines – and put the Roman camp to the sword. A second larger expedition met the same fate, and the number flocking to Spartacus's side only grew as shepherds and itinerant farmers stood side-by-side with slaves on the hills.

The growing problem for Spartacus was very like the one Hannibal faced. He was a brilliant soldier, an inspirational leader, usually able to come up with a solution to problems others thought intractable. But he, too, was a general who had a cause but not an aim. Hannibal wanted to force Rome to agree a lasting peace with Carthage, something that the Romans' own stubborn refusal to give in made impossible. Spartacus had an army with fire in its belly through the Romans' ill-treatment of slaves, the poor and farmhands displaced by *latifundia*. But his search for an endgame was even more difficult, since his polyglot followers came from all over Europe and could never agree what exactly they were fighting for.

The defeat of the Romans? Impossible.

The creation of an independent state headed by Spartacus, embracing the regions that had so recently rebelled in the Social War? Unlikely too, given that Rome had offered citizenship to those same regions, and they had little reason to reject the devil they knew for a different devil who was once a slave.

Perhaps Spartacus wanted nothing more than to go home to Thrace with his fellow countrymen and ex-gladiators. To see the back of Rome forever. At one point he moved north as if he hoped to cross the mountains and make such a journey. But then he turned back. Later he began a march on Rome and changed his mind again. The details of his movements are hazy but seem to involve raids as far apart as Nola in Campania and Thurii close to Tarentum, probably because the slave army had now splintered into different factions.

Two years on, after a series of ever more embarrassing defeats, Rome knew it was now engaged in a real war, one on its own territory, threatening the fragile hold it had on key cities after so many recent upheavals. The tide only turned when they gave the leadership of a new army to Sulla's old protégé Crassus.

He was in a good position for the job. With his seemingly limitless wealth, he could afford to pay for his troops' weapons, training and food out of his own pocket, cannily making them his own for the future. At their head, he set out to push Spartacus's army south, through Lucania, trapping them in the toe of Italy with no escape. Though the first he'd kill would be his own.

~

ALL OVER EUROPE archaeological digs have uncovered hard evidence that individual Romans had the same kind of feelings for their loved ones we take for granted today. The grave of a child along the Via Appia on the outskirts of Rome has a message that reads 'terra sis illi laevis fuit illa tibi'. *Earth sit gently on her, as she was with you.* It was a common gravestone sentiment adapted from a Greek tragedy, used for sons and daughters, for wives perhaps lost to childbirth. The men who left them might be soldiers who would go on campaign knowing they could be ordered to enter cities to kill, rape and plunder as one of the perks of the job. Then afterwards, if they had the chance, return to their families and the kind of domestic harmony Roman poets praised as an ideal.

Cruelty, vicious and heartless, was a weapon of the Roman state, used against enemies within and without alike. It was culturally acceptable as entertainment too in arenas where men like Spartacus would fight and die to amuse the crowd. At times, the public were horrified by the extent of that brutality. In the arena they would vote for a life to be spared if they thought the losing victim deserved a degree of sympathy. Still, there was always a divide between duty to family and duty to state. It was the state that usually won.

Crassus, by now, was boasting he was the richest man in Rome. He'd got there through the favouritism of the late Sulla and a series of dodgy property deals. One trick he'd invented, beset as Rome was with blazes among the cramped terraces of wooden houses, was the creation of its first fire brigade. They would turn up to a house or business on fire and offer to buy the place at well below the going rate. If the owner accepted they put out the flames and paid up. If he refused, they watched it burn to the ground.

Domestically, Crassus seemed to have a stable family life, two sons, a wife, Tertulla, to whom he was faithful. The gossips said she took lovers, among them Crassus's younger fellow politician Julius Caesar, but he seemed not to mind. Cruelty was something Crassus appears to have kept for when he felt it was needed. As he set off to put down the Spartacus rebellion, it would be directed first against his own men.

An advance force had been dispatched with orders to slow down Spartacus's forces without engaging them. Keen for battle, they fought anyway — and lost. A furious Crassus revived the vicious form of military punishment known as 'decimation'. Five hundred of the survivors were forced to choose lots. A tenth of those — hence 'decimation' — selected were then bludgeoned to death in front of the whole army. Crassus was determined his troops would fear him more than they feared the rebels. Spartacus, in return, crucified a captured Roman soldier to give his men the same message, a foreshadowing of what lay ahead down the road.

It's easy to tut-tut and shake your head at the savagery of these Romans. But the British were putting their own soldiers and even a few officers in front of firing squads a century ago in the First World War on the grounds of cowardice. The record for killing your own in that conflict, however, rests with the Italian army chief of staff Luigi Cadorna who routinely executed officers and men for incompetence or failure in the field, and had a habit of shooting any stragglers late back from the front.

Crassus, in all probability, had no need to inflict decimation upon his troops. He was pitting trained soldiers against a ragtag makeshift army, with time and geography on his side. Steadily, the tide turned against the rebellion that began with the escape of seventy or so slave gladiators from close to the arena in Capua. Now they may have numbered 70,000, but more resembled a travelling caravan than an organised, trained army. Crassus pushed Spartacus further and further south towards Rhegium, the very toe of Italy. Here a short boat ride could have taken the rebels across the Strait of Messina to Sicily and, perhaps, escape. But the pirates paid to provide the boats never arrived. While Spartacus waited, trapped, news came that other forces were coming to join Crassus. Pompey was headed from Spain. A further Roman army had landed at Brundisium after a successful campaign in Thrace and was marching south too.

As Spartacus saw the net tightening around him, Crassus moved.

This was a victory he wanted for himself, no one else. Being sole victor would stand him in good stead back home. The site of the final battle remains a mystery. All we know is that Crassus's army met Spartacus's forces somewhere in the upper valley of the Sele river in Campania, not far from the Via Popilia running from Capua to Rhegium. Close by, too, was the site of a battle Hannibal had fought after lifting a siege of Capua, one in which the Romans had been routed. Crassus was determined he would face no such ignominy.

It was the spring of 71 BC. Spartacus and his band of gladiators, runaway slaves, deserters, peasants, criminals and their families had been wandering Italy for two years, fighting a diminishing guerrilla war, plundering where they could, picking up stragglers who wanted to join them. As an old soldier he must have known this could only end one way. Before the battle, Spartacus drew his horse to him and cut its throat. If they won the day he'd have plenty of fresh horses to choose from, he said. If he lost, he'd have no need of a horse at all.

Fifteen hundred years later, on a muddy field at Towton in Yorkshire, Richard Neville, Earl of Warwick, 'the Kingmaker', was wounded, leading his Yorkist army into a decisive battle against the Lancastrian forces of Henry VI. He too slaughtered his horse in front of his troops and declared, 'Let him fly that will, for surely I will tarry with him that will tarry with me.'

Someone, you suspect, had done his reading of history. Warwick won, for a while anyway. Spartacus wasn't so lucky. In the heat of battle, probably sensing it was lost, he plunged into the midst of the fighting looking to reach Crassus, a barbarian performing the act of *devotio*, sacrificing himself for the greater cause. But any gods he was calling on were foreign ones, deaf to the cries of the slaughtered in Campania. Centurions cut him down long before he could reach their general.

With their leader gone, the rebels soon lost hope. There was no roundup of chained prisoners, each of them crying 'I'm Spartacus'. That was the invention of Stanley Kubrick. The Romans slaughtered everyone who stood their ground then set out in pursuit of those who'd fled the field. The body of the real Spartacus was never found.

A rebellion that began with a handful of gladiators dashing for freedom in Capua and turned into a war that shook Italy was over. One last public act of cruelty awaited and Crassus was determined no one who saw it would ever forget.

THE MEN and women around Spartacus had little to lose. If they were gladiators, they might have died in the arena, fighting a wild animal or one of their peers, perhaps a friend. Peasants, slaves, deserting soldiers... they were all leading lives of misery and servitude and could guess what they faced if Crassus captured them in defeat.

The Roman army chased the survivors north, sweeping up the men and women fleeing amidst the fields and high ground leading towards Capua. By the time they reached the city they had an army of miserable captives trudging over the cobbles in chains. Some might have hoped they'd be whipped then sent back to their masters in the fields. That had happened with slave revolts before, out of a need for manual labour, not forgiveness. It wasn't to be. There, in the city where the revolt began, Crassus ordered a performance of public torture and savagery like nothing even brutal Italy had seen before.

Six thousand prisoners were crucified along the entire Via Appia all the way to Rome. The exact details we don't know – on a single side of the road or both? But the maths are easy. If it was one side there was a cross with a victim on it every hundred feet or so. If it was both make that two hundred. None of the thousands of travellers along the most famous road in Italy would miss this nightmare spectacle. Every section carried its share of bodies on the cross, from Capua to the coast through Minturnae, Formia, Tarracina, inland to the Alban Hills and Aricia then along the dead-straight line of Appius's original road, today's most well-trodden remaining part, that pretty, touristy section leading out from the Porta San Sebastiano.

Some would be nailed to their wooden cross. Others tied there, ankles and wrists, and left to starve. Their corpses stayed on view for years, rotting, pecked at as carrion by birds, reduced in the end to bones, a warning to everyone who passed: this is what happens if you rise against Rome. This is the fate that awaits you however long it takes.

As the Via Appia makes its way into Rome, there's a tomb there still, a huge circular, drum-like structure at the three-mile marker, that has an odd connection to this ghastly interlude, one that appalled a good number of Romans at the time. It's a popular tourist spot, one of the best-preserved of the many mausolea along this pretty stretch of the Via Appia, much painted and photographed over the years. The position was chosen very carefully. Like the mausoleum of the Scipios on the other side of the Porta San Sebastiano, it was there to impose its presence upon all passing travellers, to let them know they were in the ghostly presence of a family as close to royalty as republican Rome would allow.

Within that circular tomb once lay the remains of the noblewoman Caecilia Metella, daughter-in-law to Marcus Licinius Crassus. A child of ten or so when he had his men start hammering those dread wooden piles into the earth beside the road where one day she would be buried. Perhaps she even saw their rotting remains on that grim line of crosses stretching out to the Alban Hills in the distance.

Crassus enjoyed his cruelty to the full. Still, it didn't give him the victory he craved.

THE SPARTACUS REVOLT RATTLED ROME. What they'd thought at first was the nuisance of a pesky bunch of outlaws turned, in the end, into a real war, one in which leading politicians and generals lost their lives alongside thousands of soldiers. When the fog of battle finally cleared, while the victims of the crucifixions along the Via Appia were still rotting by the roadside, it became obvious that Pompey, Crassus's emerging rival, would be the one to steal the honours from the man who'd really won the campaign. Pompey's forces had come across five thousand or so followers of Spartacus fleeing north and slaughtered the lot. Crassus may have fought the larger and more bloody battle in Campania but it was his political adversary who got his propaganda in first, writing to the Senate that, 'in open battle, indeed, Crassus had conquered the slaves, but that he himself had stamped out the war'. The subliminal message to the Roman people was a simple one: Crassus was good at putting down the scum of runaway slaves, but Pompey was the one winning victories abroad, then racing back to Italy to finish the job others hadn't quite completed.

Rivalry and riches were at the heart of the Roman Republic now, with Caesar joining these two in an unlikely alliance in which honour and military power, money and influence were shared among them, while at the edges Cicero watched and analysed and tried to pull the strings.

The stage was set for the next shift in Roman history, a revolution that would be the most fundamental since the end of the monarchy four centuries before.

❧ 9 ❧

LIFE BEYOND THE WARS

HOW MUCH DID the high politics of Rome matter to the man on the equivalent of the Via Appia omnibus? We don't know. History was written for and by the upper classes, frequently massaged to suck up to whoever happened to be in power at the time. The thoughts and fears of ordinary mortals never came into it. Why bother? Most of them could barely read.

Rome saw itself as the world's finest example of a functioning military and economic state, and the leading men – all men, of course – who steered the ship were the only individuals worthy of serious judgement. Throughout the histories of the time you'll find references to 'nobility'. Even in some of the most critical biographies of leading figures, writers will often attempt to find a few elements of their character to praise, as if it was unthinkable that any great Roman could be without some redeeming quality, however bloodthirsty and tyrannical they happened to be. Spartacus, as well, came to be lauded as an impressive enemy, capable of a kind of slave nobility. Though perhaps this was simply a way of excusing the fact he'd inflicted such painful and worrying blows upon the Roman state. How could a mere gladiator have achieved that if he was simply a lowborn barbarian?

Great generals on both sides returned the ashes of important enemy officers killed on the battlefield after cremating them with full military honours, and the histories made sure to record the fact. Meanwhile, the dead of the ranks were counted in uncertain numbers and thrown into unmarked mass graves, serving soldiers whipped or executed over disciplinary issues while civilians unfortunate enough to be caught in falling cities were simply collateral to dissuade others from resisting Rome's might.

Yet for all the constant conflicts life went on, and the Via Appia got busier and busier. Soldiers, diplomats, spies and crooks, farmers from the vineyards and fields of Campania and, more and more, traders from afar, moving to and from the ports of Brundisium and Tarentum, travelled up and down the road, for commerce, for diplomacy, for advancement and leisure. Rome was slowly turning cosmopolitan, developing a taste for the exotic, in food, in culture too.

MINTURNAE IS one of those archaeological sites you can never quite picture until you turn up. It's somewhere with oodles of history and plenty to see. Will there be lines of coaches outside and more fake centurions with plastic swords? Only one way to find out.

The place lies close to the coast just inside Lazio by the Garigliano river marking the border with Campania. The Via Appia got there early, so it was a Roman colony by 296 BC, soon a busy centre of commerce, feeding goods north, south and inland to Capua thirty miles away. Since the road ran right through the centre, it saw its share of passing military activity over the centuries. In the fallout of the Social War, Sulla chased his great enemy Marius across the nearby marshes. When the town captured Marius it sentenced him to death. There followed one of those odd stories Plutarch throws in from time to time. When the soldier tasked with the execution walked in to face the famous general the old man looked up and demanded, 'Would you kill Marius?' The soldier, a 'barbarian' Plutarch notes, as if that explains everything, panicked at the presence of the famous military man and fled his presence, crying he couldn't possibly go through with the judicial murder. Neither could the locals so they let the fortunate Marius go.

There's a marvellous painting by a student of David, Jean Germain Drouais, in the Louvre entitled *Marius at Minturnae* with the cowed soldier cloaking his face in fear as the stern old general stares up at him, arm outstretched, helmet by his side. It's a severe, neo-classicist masterpiece by an artist who might have become more famous had he not died in Rome at the age of twenty five. His Marius would scare the life out of me.

Not that there's anything severe or terrifying about Minturnae today. I was only the second car to park there on a sultry Thursday afternoon. When it came to locating someone who could sell me a ticket I had to find the attendant myself. He was having a jolly lunch with his family in the garden behind the office. There are a lot of archaeological sites along the length of the Via Appia, as one might expect. Only the hardened follower of ruins will visit more than a handful. But Minturnae definitely goes on the list. The old road still runs straight through the centre of the site, serving as its *decumanus*. Well-kept and with a shiny cobbled surface to walk along, it feeds into what was once a very typical Roman town with a forum, temples, a large bath complex, a market and an area thought to be where the *tabernae,* shops selling food, drink and other goods, stood, beneath the living accommodation of the people who ran them.

There'd be rooms to let and the kind of entertainment you imagine our poet friend Horace would greatly appreciate. The nearby river, then known as the Liris, was cited for its beauty in Roman poetry and there was a sacred wood, dedicated to a mysterious nymph, which was good for the local tourist trade. It's a delightful spot on any itinerary for the Via Appia. But to see beyond the stones and the ruins into life here you need to step inside the small museum beneath the seats of the amphitheatre. Here you can find revealed what kept Minturnae going – commerce. The port nearby was primarily used for shipping goods. That meant vessels capable of carrying between a hundred and a hundred and fifty tonnes long distances, and in relatively short periods if the weather was fine.

An example of how swift shipping was in this new world of

international trade comes from a famous old grump, Cato the Elder. He's best known as the politician who begged for war with Carthage by ending every speech he gave to the Senate – and there were plenty – with the words, 'Carthage must be destroyed.' Cato was no stranger to the Via Appia. He'd served as an officer in Capua and taken part in the recapture of Tarentum from Hannibal. Addressing the Senate once again on the need to raze Carthage to the ground, he dropped some figs from his toga as if by accident. When his peers admired the quality and freshness of the fruit he pointed out they'd been picked only three days before, in Africa. That, Cato insisted, was how close Carthage was to Rome, all the more reason why the city should be attacked.

It was theatre, of course, and no one knows if those figs really did come from the other side of the Mediterranean. But in the right conditions trading ships of the day could make the journey in that time, landing their cargo at Ostia for transport directly into the city along the Tiber.

In Minturnae's compact museum there's a comprehensive display of how the business of food and goods distribution worked. For starters the Romans were firm believers in fixed prices set by the state – and inflicted severe penalties, including execution, on those who tried to get round the law. In the *macellum* outside, produce would be divided into fish, meat and vegetable stalls, just like an Italian market today, with steaming terracotta pots offering the Roman equivalent of fast food to the hungry. The most essential item in any working class household – grain for bread – was subsidised by the state, a handout that caused politicians and emperors no end of trouble from time to time.

The earliest example of a cookery book, written by Apicius in the first century AD, lists a vast number of recipes for all kinds of fish, game, fruits and vegetables. Dishes such as ostrich with pepper, mint, cumin, leeks, celery seed, dates, honey, vinegar, and raisin wine were strictly for the toffs. Olive oil was for everyone, however, and would be subsidised on occasion too.

As for wine... the Roman aristocracy were oenophiles of the highest order and loved the stuff. Grumpy Cato owned extensive farmlands and vineyards and wrote a treatise on how to make good wine. A vineyard equivalent to seventy five hectares would, he declared, require 'an overseer, a housekeeper, ten labourers, one teamster, one muleteer, one willow-worker, one swineherd — a total of sixteen persons; two oxen and two draft donkeys'. In case the landowners of Roman times were in any doubt, he also makes it clear how important it was to sell on sickly slaves before they became a burden.

The upper classes would drink wine aged in clay amphorae for years, just like fine vintages today. Recycling was not an option. Once used an amphora could never be refilled. You'll find them in museums everywhere throughout Italy, Minturnae among them. In Rome the wine was shipped ashore at Emporio, the port next to modern Testaccio. An entire small terraced hill there, the Monte dei Cocci – the 'mountain of shards' – is actually a Roman era rubbish dump, made up of millions upon millions of broken amphorae thrown away after use. Today popular bars and restaurants surround this artificial hill, a few using its shards as decoration.

The best-known ancient wine was Falernian beloved of emperors and aristocrats everywhere. It came from the Monte Massico region south of the Via Appia as it headed towards Capua and was made with that early red grape we now call Aglianico, or perhaps a predecessor of it. Pricey stuff as a sign in a Pompeii bar illustrated...

For one as (a coin) you can drink wine
For two you can drink the best
For four you can drink Falernian.

There were lots of others to try. Greek historian Strabo listed some of the many types available in the region from the Pontine Marshes to Monte Massico.

The Caecuban Plain borders on the Gulf of Caietas; and next to the plain comes Fundi (Fondi), situated on the Via Appia. All these places produce exceedingly good wine; indeed, the Caecuban and the Fundanian and the Setinian belong to the class of wines that are widely famed, as is the case with the Falernian and the Alban and the Statanian.

Horace, clearly something of a wine connoisseur, made his preferences known very clearly more than once, and it wasn't for the Falernian everyone else loved. His favourites were from Cales (Calvi Risorta), north of Capua, and the Caecuban from near modern Fondi recommended by Strabo. In an ode to his chum Maecenas, he wrote...

> For you Calenian grapes are press'd,
> And Caecuban; these cups of mine
> Falernum's bounty ne'er has bless'd,
> Nor Formian vine.

THERE'S no way of knowing what kind of wine, cheap or posh, once sat in those terracotta amphorae propped up in museums everywhere today. It's just obvious Romans liked it... a lot. Wandering around the exhibits in Minturnae, all tucked beneath the seats where the locals once enjoyed theatre and gladiatorial shows, you find yourself surrounded by the remains of that lost age, headless statues, milestones, signs, shattered pottery, the decorated capitals of vanished columns, recovered beams from trading vessels, mostly documented and explained with great care.

The poets must have been right in thinking Minturnae a pleasant stop along the Via Appia. Cicero was a fan too, mentioning it in his letters. He had a seaside villa in Puteoli in the Bay of Naples and an estate just north in Formia, so he was doubtless a frequent visitor. Rich or poor, Minturnae was a welcome break from the febrile politics of the big city where riots and mob killings over politics were common in the heated times that followed the fall of Spartacus.

The Italy that now lay under Roman rule was nothing like the patchwork quilt of tribes and malleable, would-be nations of Appius's time. It was connected, by transport, by commerce, by the authoritarian rule that ran out from Rome along the cobbles of its expanding network of highways, defined still by cultures that sometimes got on and sometimes clashed. Even with a new-found citizenship for most,

Italy was argumentative and divided, tribe against tribe, family against family, ambitious politician against his peers. For those working the levers of power in the capital there was also the abiding memory of Sulla, someone who'd risen from near-poverty to break the mould of centuries of Roman tradition, tearing up the idea that one man could never rule alone.

Sulla's lesson was that a single, determined individual, with an army behind him and enough money, could march straight into the centre of Rome and seize power from consuls and the Senate, perhaps even establish a new monarchy. Crassus, Pompey and Caesar duly took note, as did Cicero, scribbling down everything as it happened and never sparing anyone with his opinion on matters large and small.

Yet the prize would elude them all, as would a peaceful end. To see the true winner we need to find a barrel-chested, armour-clad, heroic figure among the headless statues in Minturnae. It was probably an inaccurate representation, not that anyone would have dared say such a thing while he was alive. This was the man who finally won the crown of Rome, the outsider who, as a teenager, came out of the shadows after chasing some of the last remnants of Spartacus's defeated followers along the Via Appia.

When that was done he took the boat from Brundisium and crossed the Adriatic to study with a Greek tutor in Apollonia. He came to know Minturnae well over the years and paid for some of those ruins we see today.

But, in 44 BC, when he first enters this story he's just eighteen, scared, short of cash, going by the name Gaius Octavius Thurinus.

The night I had to dodge round all those happy basketball fans by the harbour in Brindisi I was walking where he must have stood two millennia before, at the last mile of the Via Appia, a road he'd taken months earlier, thinking only of his bright future ahead in the military. Now Gaius Octavius Thurinus suspected with good reason he was a marked man, a rich price on his head for anyone who'd deliver it to those who'd just assassinated Julius Caesar in Rome.

Standing by the sparkling blue waters of the Adriatic, counting his odds of survival, there's a letter in his hands from his mother and stepfather in the capital. Before he was murdered Caesar wrote a will and named him as his adoptive son and heir. A gift that's as good as a death sentence, which is why his stepfather is pleading with him to forget it and accept a quiet, safe life of anonymity instead.

What's a lad to do?

❦ III ❧

THE AGE OF EMPERORS

Imperial statue, Brindisi museum.

❧ 10 ❧

OCTAVIAN GROWS UP... QUICKLY

WHAT A LAD DID WAS FOLLOW his nature. As one of his biographers put it a few decades later: *he already had his mind on great things*. This eighteen-year-old in peril took his time and set about saving his own skin then climbing the bloody ladder of ambition. He wrote back to his stepfather to say he was accepting his adoption and changing his name to that of his newly assassinated adoptive father, Gaius Julius Caesar. Though just to make things complicated (this is Roman history) most people from that point on called him Octavian for a while, and so shall I until we get to the point where there's another twist in the tale.

After that he persuaded the local officials and military in Brundisium – all of whom it turned out were admirers of Caesar – to back his cause, and hand over the war chests of funds that had been sent to the region to pay for a coming campaign against the Parthians in the east. Octavian then set off up the Via Appia, accompanied by happy veterans with more money in their pockets than they had before, and plenty of reasons to recruit their fellow soldiers to their young leader's cause as he marched north into Campania, a region that had always had a soft spot for his murdered so-called dad.

On May the sixth, 44 BC, just six weeks after the Ides of March when the daggers of Brutus, Cassius and his fellow assassins took Caesar's life, he arrived in a tense and dangerous Rome, a callow, largely unknown and impoverished teenager no more. But note this. On March the fifteenth, when Caesar was murdered, the then Octavius was in Apollonia on the other side of the Adriatic, in modern Albania. Within the space of six weeks he was able to hear the news from Rome, sail for Italy, gather forces and funds in Brundisium and march north, some three hundred and fifty miles, three thousand soldiers by his side.

This was the new Roman state, sophisticated, mobile, filled with a highly trained and ruthless military available to the highest bidder, divided politically by warring factions that more and more were fighting out their differences in battles on the street and across the land. The teenage Octavian was about to step into a sea of dangers, and would soon turn for advice to a voluble and clever man who'd been in the midst of the last two decades of fiery politics along the length of Italy and beyond into the Mediterranean at large.

11

THE VIEW FROM THE COAST

FORMIA IS A JOLLY little seaside town in southern Lazio. The Via Appia there is a busy modern road bringing trippers from Rome attracted by the beaches, the bars, the sailing and the inexpensive restaurants. Ferries leave for Ponza in the Pontine islands, much as they would have done two millennia ago. With wonderful views to Ischia on the edge of the Bay of Naples and, across the gulf the imposing headland of Gaeta, the place has always had a holiday air about it. 'Sweet Formiae,' wrote the poet Martial. 'Here is no stagnant sea or air.'

The odd smelly two-stroke moped apart, the air's as sweet as ever today, though the town itself was badly damaged during Allied landings in the Second World War. Still, Roman remains lurk everywhere. At low tide you can find traces of fish ponds where the local aristocrats raised mullet and lamprey, for the table and also as a kind of pet. Behind the town, hidden away on a side street, is a vast Roman cistern used to store water, now restored and open to visitors a few hours a day.

On that rocky promontory of Gaeta there's a real rarity: a circular Roman tomb that, for once, can be linked directly to the individual who was once interred within. He was Lucius Munatius Plancus, a wily aristocrat who changed sides as it suited him during the turbulent times we're about to enter. Fans of Robert Graves and *I, Claudius* may remember his daughter Plancina, wife to the treacherous Piso who poisons poor, noble Germanicus on the orders of Augustus's wife Livia then later commits suicide. The Livia part is based on Roman gossip but the rest seems true. According to the historian Suetonius, her father Plancus was the sycophant who in 27 BC, at the close of this section of our journey, proposed Octavian be renamed 'Augustus', an obscure and ancient religious term variously translated as 'exalted', 'serene' and 'venerable'. An act that very definitely brought about the end of the Roman republic and began the age of emperors. Everyone said Plancus was a creep, but a creep who at least left us the name of a month.

Formia boasts a well-stocked museum with funeral monuments, frescoes and stucco work all retrieved from excavated private villas along the coast, as well as the inevitable busts of Augustus and Livia. He certainly had close connections to the place and must have spent some time with family there. His stepfather, Lucius Marcius Philippus, who wrote that letter telling him to keep his head down and ignore Caesar's will, had a villa here, the ruins of it supposedly still visible in the smart Villa Irlanda hotel on the way to Gaeta. Or so I read while lounging by the Irlanda's pool measuring out the days I had left before I had to be back handing over the car at Fiumicino.

Philippus was a close chum of Formia's most famous resident, a man remembered in the name given to a stretch of the Via Appia here: Via Marco Tullio Cicerone. The statesman, writer, orator, gossip and general know-it-all we call Cicero. Villa Rubino, between the port and the beach, on the busy Viale Unità D'Italia, is thought to occupy the spot where he kept a seaside home. It was one of his many country estates since Cicero was a wealthy self-made man who'd climbed to the top of the tree of Rome through his skill as a lawyer and political wheeler-dealer. His private palace in ancient Formiae stretched to five acres or so though now there's just a rather decrepit elderly mansion in its place. There's little to show from the outside that it was once the site of a grand Roman residence and later, in the nineteenth century, a seaside palace for Ferdinand II, King of the Two Sicilies (in other words both the kingdoms of Sicily and Naples). There's talk of taking it into public ownership and continuing with earlier excavations which have uncovered traces of fishponds, a nymphaeum, terraces, a fountain and a small harbour. I wouldn't hold your breath. Schemes like this are in limbo everywhere in Italy, and the economic woes of late aren't likely to improve their chances of happening. This is a country where it's hard to turn a spade without uncovering something that makes an archaeologist faint with passion. Right now the old home of one of ancient Rome's most famous citizens lies beneath an ugly crumbling ruin with no public access to the grounds.

Cicero was both participant and spectator to the events that followed the death of Sulla, fundamental changes in the nature of the Roman state and how it was to be governed. He was a man with towering ambitions, to lead and further the interests of Rome wherever he could. A traditionalist who was opposed to any one individual having power longer than the consular system allowed, though you have to wonder whether he might have changed his opinion on that if he was the one being given the chance.

HE WAS BORN in Arpinum (Arpino) on the slow road to Benevento, the Via Latina, in 106 BC. After studying law at Rome, the young Cicero embarked on a journey becoming popular with upper class Romans of an intellectual bent, the sea crossing from Brundisium to Athens and Rhodes. This was a little like an Eton and Oxbridge education for the young of the time. Many were dispatched upon it to learn rhetoric, philosophy and the arts of public speaking, the latter so necessary back home for anyone wishing to join the ceaseless debating society of the Senate. Cicero so approved of Greece for education that he was to send his own son, Marcus, to Athens where the young man fell into the company of Horace, our poet from Venusia, and largely indulged himself in drink and debauchery. Horace sobered up and found better things to do. Marcus, to his father's annoyance, remained something of a disappointment.

Cicero had firm opinions about military matters but no zest to race to the front with a sword himself. When Sulla was busy seizing the reins of Rome he made himself scarce with another trip to the east – to stay out of the dictator's way, according to Plutarch, though Cicero insisted it was for his health. By 63 BC, at the age of forty three, he'd climbed so far up the political ladder he'd been elected Consul with the help of the Optimates, standing as a traditionalist determined to oppose the political reforms of the Populares. His year in office was full of excitement. Cicero claimed that a rival Populares politician, Catiline, was planning revolution in the city and gave a series of famous speeches known as the Catiline Orations in which he castigated his rival face-to-face in the Senate. Parts remain famous today, such as Cicero declaring, '*O tempora, o mores!*' Oh, what times! Oh, what behaviour!

Catiline knew when his number was up and legged it with some of his conspirators. Those foolish enough to remain in Rome were controversially executed on Cicero's express orders – something he'd pay for later – and Catiline himself was wiped out with his army soon after.

Cicero was, by now, firmly in the top echelon of Roman society, owner of a fancy house on the Palatine Hill he'd bought from Crassus, on intimate terms with Pompey and Caesar too, confidant, if not necessarily a trusted one, to the three men wrestling with one another for control of the growing Roman Empire.

In 60 BC that bickering trio formed an informal alliance known as the First Triumvirate in which they agreed to divide power between them, a deal to avoid the possibility of civil war. So important was Cicero by now that he was invited to join it, but refused on the grounds that the pact was against the spirit of the republic. A year later his star was very abruptly on the wane. The triumvirate persuaded a dodgy politician called Publius Clodius Pulcher to hound him into exile for ordering the execution of the Catiline conspirators. A screaming mob, paid by Clodius, burned down his beautiful house on the Palatine. In Greece he lingered, a depressed figure seemingly lost as the uneasy alliance between the three leaders of the triumvirate hovered on the brink of civil war.

It took the intervention of another dodgy politician, Titus Annius

Milo, to arrange for his return to Rome. Cicero duly landed back at Brundisium and took the familiar journey north in August 57 BC. When the likes of Crassus, Pompey and Caesar made that trip they did so accompanied by thousands of their own loyal troops, willing to die for the men who paid them. But Cicero was now an outsider, happier with his books and his writing than the ever more violent hurly-burly of politics in the city. His enemy, the thuggish Clodius, was furious he'd returned, and set his bully boys to attacking the workmen rebuilding his house on the Palatine, once even attacking the timid Cicero himself in the street.

Riven by vendettas, terrorised by roaming rival gangs day and night, Rome was on edge as the fragile alliance between Crassus, Pompey and Caesar teetered on the verge of collapse. A chance encounter on the Via Appia would soon place Cicero in its midst.

TEN MILES OUTSIDE ROME, not far from the ugly sprawl of Ciampino airport, a charming cobbled stretch of the Via Appia meets the modern SS7 opposite a McDonald's drive-thru. Another mile on all traces of the historic road vanish beneath semi-rural villas and the verdant fields of small farms. Here, two thousand years ago, stood the road town of Bovillae, a busy stopping place on the way to and from the Alban Hills. There are ruins still, but all on private property so you can only look at them through satellite images.

One cold January day in 52 BC Clodius was returning with a group of slaves from an outing to Aricia in the hills. Perhaps on political business. Or maybe to eat the famous meat from there – modern Ariccia is still regarded as one of the finest places in Italy to find the archetypal roast pork dish, *porchetta*. Milo was coming the other way with a party of gladiators and guards, headed for Lanuvium (Lanuvio) to appoint a priest. The two men had been bitter enemies for years, and their gangs had come to deadly blows time after time. This would be the last.

Insults flew between the two parties as they passed. A fight broke out among the rival slaves and guards. Clodius was wounded, dragged to an inn, probably not far from that McDonald's today. There Milo's gladiators dragged the wounded man out into the road and on his orders finished the fellow off.

All hell broke loose in Rome. Clodius's supporters carried his body to the Curia, the home of the Senate, and burnt the place down. Pompey, himself an intended victim of one of Clodius's assassination plots, was made sole Consul. To try to restore order he put Milo on trial for murder... and Cicero duly stood up as defence counsel.

The speech Cicero wrote for the case, known as the Pro Milone, still exists, long and meandering it is too, almost twenty thousand words in all. He makes no attempt to deny that Milo was behind the murder, though he does try to make a strong case that Clodius – travelling without his wife for once – knew he'd find Milo on the road and actually planned to assassinate him. But Cicero never got the chance to make his case. The trial was abandoned when he felt so intimidated by the mob of Clodius's supporters glaring at him and yelling threats that he was unable to give his usual eloquent address.

Milo was found guilty on a majority verdict and sent in exile to Massilia (Marseille), a place he enjoyed for the food and wine. According to Cassius Dio, Cicero only wrote his defence, Pro Milone, after the case was over and sent it to Milo whiling away his time in the south of France. Milo wrote back and joked that he was glad Cicero had never managed to deliver the oration; if he had, Milo might not have found himself lucky enough to be dining on fresh mullet in Massilia.

Cicero didn't mind losing so much. His arch-enemy, Clodius, was dead. Pompey, the oligarch he felt closest to, had the upper hand. And by now Crassus, the third member of that triumvirate, was off the scene for good.

TWO YEARS before Milo was finishing off Clodius on the Via Appia, Crassus was back in Brundisium, a huge fleet and army under his command, waiting to sail to Syria where he was to be the new governor. He was sixty. All the money, all the victories over enemies like Spartacus, had brought him to the summit of Roman politics. But

Pompey and Caesar shared that space too, and on the side Crassus was privately supporting Clodius in his baiting of Cicero and lately Pompey. Dangerous times so, in a tense conference at Luca (Lucca), the three men agreed to discuss their differences.

Caesar was in the ascendant after a successful campaign in Gaul. Crassus and Pompey were growing ever more wary of him. Like Mafia godfathers carving up territory, they struck a deal. Caesar could keep Gaul for a further five years. Pompey would control the Iberian peninsula, Hispania, from Rome. Crassus had Syria all to himself for five years. Syria meaning the east, territories rich with gold and loot, something that Crassus still lusted after, all the more since his popularity in Rome was on the wane.

Swift, straight military roads like the Via Appia meant armies could avoid the sea as much as possible. Weather, pirates, and poor navigation only added to the risks of campaigns. Crassus, though, was a man in a hurry and set off in the middle of winter, ignoring warnings of storms. He lost countless ships and men but looted everywhere he went, from Mesopotamia to the temples of Jerusalem. A still greater treasure lay before him, Parthia, modern Iran, a nation largely a mystery to the Romans but known to be rich and, so Crassus thought, ripe for the taking.

He hastened to war and was soon joined by his son Publius. In May 53 BC they met the forces of the Parthian general Surena at Carrhae, close to modern Harran in Turkey near the Syrian border. All his military skills failed the old man. Publius, wounded, facing defeat, committed suicide. Crassus met with Surena to discuss a truce, only for the talks to end in a violent argument. He was cut down in the aftermath, along with twenty thousand of his men, and a further ten thousand captured. The Parthians brought his severed head as a trophy to their king, Orodes. He ordered it to be used as a prop in a play, and according to one account – which may well be the invention of an imaginative historian – demanded molten gold be poured down his dead throat to deliver to Crassus the riches he so craved.

Plutarch concluded...

*With such a farce as this the expedition of Crassus is said to have closed, just
like a tragedy.*

Still, Crassus loved pomp and theatre, and he did go out in a way
that would later inspire a scene in *Game of Thrones*. The triumvirate was
over. Now it was just Pompey and Caesar contesting the throne of
Rome, with Cicero watching, a worried spectator in the wings.

ON JANUARY 10, 49 BC the threatening storm of civil war finally
broke. After plundering and conquering much of Gaul, Caesar's forces
crossed the Rubicon – a river now lost to us – entering a part of Italy
over which he had no legal rule. Pompey immediately fled with most of
the Senate, down the familiar route to that well-used exit point to the
east, Brundisium. Rome was abandoned to Caesar, who arrived as a
benevolent victor, offering the hand of friendship to most, if not all.
Pompey was desperate to meet up with his legions in Greece, the only
way he felt he could hope to match Caesar's own army.

As the consular roads of Italy and beyond, the Via Appia more than
any, sounded to the march of soldiers' boots, Cicero turned out to be a
dithering, highly opinionated ringside spectator to it all. He was
temperamentally inclined to support Pompey, fearing, with good
reason, that Caesar sought to rule Rome as dictator, and would be the
death of the republican system. On the other hand – and he was very
much an 'on the other hand' sort of fellow – he was aware that Caesar
seemed quite friendly towards him personally, and a very competent
politician.

Always the one to pick the wrong side, Cicero joined Pompey in
the east, annoying all and sundry with his constant offers of advice,
both political and military. Within months Caesar was dictator of
Rome and Marc Antony, a bitter enemy of Cicero's, had been
appointed his master of horse, effectively second-in-command. One
year later, at the battle of Pharsalus, Pompey's forces were routed, and
the old man fled to Egypt where he was murdered and his head offered
to a shocked Caesar as some kind of prize.

Tail between his legs, Cicero returned to Italy, to his villas in Formiae and Campania, a wife who disliked him, to his beloved daughter Tullia, miserable in a problematic marriage. He was fortunate in that Caesar proved forgiving towards his enemies once the war had ended. Cicero was pardoned, along with many others from the Senate who'd followed Pompey across the sea from Brundisium. Among them was Marcus Julius Brutus, son of Caesar's mistress, Servilia, perhaps Caesar's illegitimate offspring. Brutus was well known to Cicero. They had properties close to one another outside Puteoli, Brutus's villa being on the beautiful island of Nisida in the Gulf of Naples, where Cicero had visited him from time to time. I searched out Nisida a while back on a trip to Naples, wondering what might remain of the home where, in all probability, Brutus plotted Caesar's murder. It's now joined to the mainland by a short road, still beautiful, but inaccessible since it's used both as a naval base and a jail for juvenile offenders. Appropriate, perhaps.

In spite of all his past difficulties, Cicero remained a charismatic figure in Roman politics, someone Caesar hoped to win to his side. It wasn't easy. As ever, he simply couldn't keep his thoughts to himself. One of the many remarkable aspects of this extraordinary man is that we can read his thoughts directly, since so many of his private letters have survived, thirty seven books of them, perhaps half his lifelong correspondence. Hardly a day seems to have gone by without him dispatching a messenger with letters for the road. They cover everything from politics to personal matters and general gossip.

Here he is writing from Brundisium to his estranged wife Terentia in Rome in 48 BC about their daughter's marriage to a dangerous individual called Dolabella...

Sorrow for the illness both of Dolabella and Tullia is an addition to my other miseries. Every single thing goes wrong, and I don't know what to think or do about anything. Pray take care of your own and Tullia's health.

And here from Formiae, in December 50 BC, writing to Titus Pomponius Atticus, his most frequent correspondent, about planning a

journey along the Via Appia while worrying about the political
situation.

> *... from Formiae I go to Tarracina on the last of December. Thence to the upper
> end of the Pomptine marsh: thence to Pompey's Alban villa: and so to Rome on
> the third, my birthday. The political crisis is causing me greater fear every day.*

A few days later he's updating Atticus on the political situation
after his meeting with Pompey.

> *We reached Formiae together, and were closeted together from two o'clock till
> evening. For your query as to the chance of a peaceful settlement, so far as I
> could tell from Pompey's full and detailed discourse, he does not even want
> peace. Pompey thinks that the constitution will be subverted even if Caesar is
> elected consul without an army; and he fancies that when Caesar hears of the
> energetic preparations against him, he will give up the idea of the consulship
> this year, and prefer to keep his army and his province. Still, if Caesar should
> play the fool, Pompey has an utter contempt for him, and firm confidence in his
> own and the state's resources.*

In 45 BC he tells Atticus about a sudden visit Caesar paid him in
Puteoli. The dictator turned up unexpectedly with two thousand men
who camped outside the villa, all expecting to be fed.

> *Well, I have no reason after all to repent my formidable guest! For he made
> himself exceedingly pleasant. But on his arrival... on the evening of the second
> day of the Saturnalia, the villa was so chock-a-block with soldiers that there
> was scarcely a dining-room left for Caesar himself to dine in. Two thousand
> men, if you please! He... was under a course of emetics, and so ate and drank
> without scruple and as suited his taste. It was a very good dinner, and well
> served.*
>
> *Besides this, the staff were entertained in three rooms in a very liberal style.
> The freedmen of lower rank and the slaves had everything they could want. But
> the upper sort had a really exotic dinner. In fact, I showed I was somebody.
> However, he is not a guest to whom one would say, "Please pop in again on your
> way back." Once is enough. We didn't say a word about politics. That's the story*

of the entertainment, or I might call it the billeting on me – trying to the temper,
but not seriously inconvenient.

The most important man in Italy, someone with the power of life and death over all, has just invited himself for dinner, and Cicero is desperate he never visits again. And, typically, proud that, 'I showed I was somebody.'

Eighteen months or so after Caesar imposed himself and his followers on Cicero in Puteoli he was dead, in one of the most notorious assassinations in history. Brutus, perhaps his son, was one of those who wielded the blade. He fled Rome with his fellow conspirators when Marc Antony seized the reins of power and looked to strike down Caesar's killers.

The learned politician in Formiae knew nothing of the plot. Plutarch says...

They kept their plans a secret from Cicero, although he was foremost among
them... They feared that the caution which time and old age had brought him,
combined with his natural timidity, and further, his habit of calculating all the
details of every enterprise so as to ensure the utmost safety, would blunt the edge
of their ardour at a crisis which demanded speed.

Or perhaps they simply thought he wasn't the best at keeping secrets. He certainly approved of Caesar's murder. Writing to one of the conspirators, Gaius Trebonius, eleven months later he crowed, 'How I could wish that you had invited me to that most glorious banquet on the Ides of March!'

Trebonius was the plotter who kept Marc Antony engaged outside the Senate meeting while Caesar was stabbed to death. By then he was in Asia Minor along with most of the other conspirators, fleeing a vengeful Marc Antony's troops. There, in 43 BC, he would be captured by none other than Cicero's son-in-law, Dolabella, tortured and beheaded. Brutus and his chums thought Caesar's blood would bring an end to dictatorship and restore the glory of the Roman Republic, with him and his cohorts in charge, of course. In fact, Caesar was rather more popular with the mob than they knew, and all it took to send his murderers fleeing into exile was a little push from Marc Antony.

Cicero had misread the mood. As the climate in Rome was moving behind Antony and his new partner in power, Marcus Aemilius Lepidus, he was still writing to Brutus from Italy, risking discovery if a messenger should be caught or betray him along the way. A few of the letters are deeply personal. After Brutus fled Italy, his wife Porcia died on that pretty island of Nisida near Puteoli. Some reports say she committed suicide in the most terrible of ways, by swallowing hot coals. Cicero wrote to her distraught widower in Macedonia telling him of his sorrow and sympathy, then adding that Brutus had to hide his grief from his troops. They needed to see they had a strong leader.

At other times he reiterated his support for the work Brutus and his fellows had done back in Rome while continuing to complain they hadn't used their daggers on others too.

After the death of Caesar and your ever memorable Ides of March, Brutus, you have not forgotten what I said had been omitted by you and your colleagues, and what a heavy cloud I declared to be hanging over the Republic. A great pest had been removed by your means, a great blot on the Roman people wiped out, immense glory in truth acquired by yourselves: but an engine for exercising kingly power had been put into the hands of Lepidus and Antony, of whom the former was the more fickle of the two, the latter the more corrupt, but both of whom dreaded peace and were enemies to quiet.

It was a dangerous game to play, all the more so when the nineteen-year-old Octavian, Caesar's adopted son and heir, turned up on his doorstep, begging for advice.

12

AN EMPEROR IN THE MAKING

It's a ten-minute walk from the ruins of the holiday home of Octavian's stepfather in the Villa Irlanda hotel to the harbour close by Cicero's old villa. A pleasant stroll past beach huts and happy holiday-makers. A seafront restaurant called La Scogliera has lovely views of the bay and Ischia, and a wood-fired pizza oven worked by a very happy chef who makes his own three-day-old dough. They were eating flatbreads with toppings in Cicero's time and before. But the first recorded use of the term 'pizza' comes from Gaeta, the larger town a couple of miles along the bay. In the tenth century AD a tenant there was ordered to deliver twelve pizzas twice a year to the local bishop, on Christmas Day and Easter Sunday.

The meals the households of Cicero and the family of Octavian shared when they met up for social and political chat by the Formia shore were probably rather more grand. Before Rome began to expand along Appius's new road most of its citizens lived off a kind of porridge with the occasional eggs and cheese. Meat and fish were for the wealthy alone. As the trading records in the museum at nearby Minturnae reveal, by the first century BC Roman aristocrats were indulging their tastes for exotic luxuries to the limit, importing food and drink from across the Mediterranean. It wasn't just that they were curious. There were social reasons too. Banquets for the wealthy were now prolonged, three-course affairs, prepared by skilled chefs. Time and again Cicero, in his letters, promises his visitors a feast if they come to dine with him. The rarer the wine, the more exotic the food, the better a man proved his superior status. He may have struggled when Caesar turned up with two thousand men expecting to be fed alongside him. But Caesar was known for having more interest in politics than dining and was taking an emetic at the time. Given the banquet was bound to end up in a basin in any case, that was an occasion when the menu was doubtless the last thing on Cicero's mind, though he still can't help boasting about how good the food was when it turned up.

Octavian had good reason to pay his old neighbour a social call. He needed allies in Rome. Cicero, in spite of his opposition to Caesar, remained an important and influential figure in the Senate. The social circle of the men who ran Rome was always small as the many links between them demonstrate so frequently. Even those on different sides of bitter argument knew one another and, at times, would bury the hatchet for a common cause.

Despite their visible differences – Cicero had approved the murder of the adoptive father who'd given Octavian a path to power – the young man sought the advice of the old Senate hand forty years his senior. The two did have at least one thing in common: they both hated Marc Antony. Cicero had fought the man for years and now was vying with him for control of Rome. Octavian soon found that Antony regarded him as a youth of no consequence and refused to let him get his hands on Caesar's bequest. There was, then, a *quid pro quo* between young and old. Cicero believed that having Octavian on his side added to his own power and influence. Octavian found Cicero's support in the Senate useful and was happy to regard him as a political mentor, even going so far as to refer to him as 'father' from time to time.

The popular mood turned in Octavian's favour. He was the adopted son of Caesar, a man the public still admired. The Senate was increasingly suspicious of Antony, fearing he was intent on seizing control of the state for himself. This tense standoff came to a head in a series of sensational speeches Cicero gave known as the 'Philippics'. In spite of the fancy title, these were mostly vicious character assassinations of Marc Antony, accusing him of everything from corruption, sexual debauchery and effeminacy to military incompetence.

With his incessant letters and political scheming, Cicero was playing an ever more dangerous game. On the one hand he was trying to act as mentor to Octavian, a ruthless figure growing into the complex world of Roman politics very quickly indeed. At the same time he was in touch with Brutus who was now in the east, trying to stay out of the way. Brutus was clearly baffled by all this scheming, complaining to Atticus, Cicero's favourite correspondent, that the old man had been taken in by the young Octavian's wiles.

In the midst of all this turmoil Antony decided Rome was getting too hot for comfort, decamped north and Octavian ventured out after him. At the time Antony's name was mud in the city and Cicero the most popular and powerful man around. It wasn't to last. Never able to keep quiet when a *bon mot* popped into his head he penned a letter to a friend declaring that, after the war with Antony was won, Octavian was to be 'laudandus, ornandus, tollendus'. This is an ancient figure of speech known as a paraprosdokian, a phrase in which the last word makes you reassess the meaning as a whole, as Cicero doubtless knew. It translates as his young 'pupil' was to be 'praised, elevated and removed'. In other words, once Octavian had performed the useful function of getting Marc Antony out of the way, he too could be taken off the scene, perhaps in the same fashion as his patron, Caesar. While Cicero was never one for violence in person, he had no qualms about demanding it as a political tool.

Unfortunately, this clever little joke turned out like one of those naughty private Twitter messages where the sender hits the public button by mistake. All those letters of his, to friends everywhere, some of them enemies of others he was corresponding with, kept dashing across Italy and beyond. It's hardly surprising a few would make their way into the wrong hands. Perhaps Cicero was so proud of them he even spread them about himself. Soon his wicked witticism was all over Rome and being repeated to Octavian.

Not that it mattered much. The young chap was already on his way to consigning his new 'father' to the past.

~

In July 43 BC Cicero was still in regular correspondence with Brutus, urging him to return to Italy and make peace with Octavian. Brutus was interested. He wrote...

> *This boy in particular... what price would he offer (suppose this were a matter of haggling) that we should procure him such power as he will of course obtain, seeing that by his goodwill we want to remain alive, and to keep our estates, and to be styled consulars! Cicero, I beg and admonish you, do not flag or lose heart; and while you ward off present evils always cast a searching glance upon future ones too lest they steal in upon you...*

Cicero replied...

> *But what grieves me most sorely at the time of writing is that when the state accepted me as surety for this stripling – one might almost call him a boy – I hardly seemed in a position to make good my promise... And yet, so I hope, I shall keep my hold even on him, in spite of opposition from many quarters. For he seems to have good natural qualities, but he is pliable at his age, and many are prepared to pervert him.*

Then he signed off...

> *...there will never be any affair in which I shall not, even at the risk of my life, speak and act in the way which I shall judge to be in accord with your wishes and in your interest.*

So many strands to the prolix web he was weaving, so many ways in which it might go wrong as he tried to stay in the good books of men who hated one another. A few weeks later, eighteen months after landing outside Brundisium, a scared and penurious teenager, Octavian was voted Consul of Rome with Cicero's backing, though he was well below the minimum age for the post. Not that the Senate had much choice. There were eight legions, paid for and very loyal to him, waiting outside the city gates; a handful had turned up at the Senate brandishing their swords in case anyone didn't get the message. Straight away Octavian demanded the passage of a law declaring Caesar's assassins criminals, and those who supported them.

Another shock was just around the corner. Far from fighting Antony, for the moment at least, Octavian decided to go into an alliance with him and Lepidus, forming a triumvirate like the one Crassus, Pompey and his 'father' had used to carve up the empire.

After that they revived something even older, the dark and deadly practice Sulla had used to terrify and murder at will in Rome while filling up the city's depleted treasury, and his own coffers. The three men sat down to draw up a list of the proscribed. Three hundred senators and two thousand knights who would be hunted down, lose their homes, their estates, their fortunes, along with their lives.

There's a story about those proscriptions that needs to be taken with that large proverbial grain of salt. Supposedly the three princes of this new second triumvirate agreed to prove their dedication to one another by sacrificing someone close to them. Lepidus added the name of his brother, Paulus, who'd opposed the new pact. Marc Antony offered his uncle, Lucius Julius Caesar, who had voted for him to be declared an enemy of state.

Octavian, supposedly after much wrangling, put down Cicero's name, doubtless to the delight of Marc Antony, still furious after the abuse heaped on him earlier in the year in the Philippics.

Paulus and Lucius managed to escape punishment and would be pardoned. Cicero must have known he was never going to get that chance.

A FEW MINUTES' walk from the table by the sea where I ate my pizza in La Scogliera, there was a private harbour for Cicero's villa. When I was there it was September, a beautiful late summer day, the water clear as a jewel, Ischia beckoning in the distance, swimmers everywhere, kids floating around on plastic inflatables. But winters here can turn brutal, and it was December when Cicero found himself in Formiae, fleeing Rome, desperate for passage out to the east where he could meet up with Brutus for the war he knew would come.

There's an air of tragedy around him now, and it's not just the fact that the 'stripling boy' he thought his pupil had turned on his mentor with a sentence of death. Cicero's beloved daughter Tullia is gone, one more woman lost to the complications of pregnancy so common at the time. She was dearer to him than anyone, and her loss depressed him deeply. Along with that must have been the knowledge that so many of his political decisions, deeply thought through, always undertaken with intense intellectual rigour, backed the wrong horse in the end. Cicero was a dyed-in-the-wool republican and would always oppose any party – Caesar, Antony, Octavian – he felt was minded to take Rome back to the days of dictators, of power resting in the hands of one man alone, lording it over the Senate for life through a brutal tyranny.

Yet whichever way he turned it seemed the republican mood he believed responsible for Rome's uniqueness and success was dying. The people had loved Caesar. They felt much the same about his adoptive son. The Senate, in any case, was a democratic process only in the sense that it represented the upper classes. The teeming masses of Rome wanted food and entertainment, the 'bread and circuses' the poet Juvenal was to write about a century and a half after Cicero was dust. The old wheeler-dealer was sixty three and there was nothing left to do but run from Italy again. Probably for the last time. The second triumvirate was in no mood to relinquish what it had.

One bitter and windy day he boarded a boat in his private harbour. It was a desperate bid to escape. The roads were controlled by the military, with orders to seize and execute him on the spot. There was no safe and easy land route to Brundisium, the obvious place to cross the Adriatic. A long sea journey seemed the only option, and even that was soon impossible. The weather had turned. The conditions were too rough. Cicero's boat was forced back to shore where he spent the night in his villa.

The following morning the soldiers arrived. Plutarch writes...

After they had broken in the door, which they found closed, Cicero was not to be seen, and the inmates said they didn't know where he was. Then a youth who'd been generously educated by Cicero, a freedman of his brother Quintus, Philologus by name, told the tribune that the litter was being carried through the wooded and shady walks towards the sea. When they saw Cicero he ordered the servants to set the litter down where they were. Then, clasping his chin with his left hand, as was his habit, he looked steadfastly at his killers, his head all squalid and unkempt, and his face wasted with anxiety, so that most of those that stood by covered their faces. He stretched his neck out from the litter and was slain.

On Antony's orders he was decapitated and the hands that wrote the Philippics were cut off. All were taken to Rome where Antony had the hands nailed to the platform used for public speeches while his wife, Fulvia, stuck golden hairpins in the dead Cicero's tongue to punish him for his words.

Up the hill from Formia, by the side of the busy modern road that follows the ancient Via Appia's tracks, is a stone building, a little like the base of a windmill. It's open rarely and there's nothing much to see to be honest. For centuries locals have told visitors this was where Cicero's ashes – such as they were – once sat in an urn. Up the hill from the site is another, more ruined tomb that's said to be that of his daughter Tullia. Historians will tell you there's no evidence to back these claims. It's possible Cicero's 'tomb' is a votive, a monument put up to honour him. All the same, the locals come to remember him there from time to time, reading his work in period costume. For all his failings, he remains one of the most famous and revered of all the ancient Romans.

The man who sentenced him to death seems to have remembered him too. Plutarch says that the ageing Augustus found one of his grandchildren reading one of Cicero's books. The boy desperately tried to hide the fact when he saw who'd walked into the room. His grandfather simply said, 'A learned man, my child, a learned man and a lover of his country.'

But by then he was a long way from the callow, scared youth who'd stood by the waterfront in Brundisium wondering if he'd make it to Rome alive. Soon the very transformation Cicero most feared would happen. Giving it a helpful push would be the poet whose ribald and roughshod journey along the Via Appia we've already encountered. Except it wasn't a jolly at all. It was a trip with a purpose.

13

A POET WITH A MISSION

HORACE WAS a fan of Cicero and might so easily have suffered the same fate. He was in Athens, studying during the day and drinking at night with Cicero's son, when Julius Caesar was murdered. Perhaps it was just convenience, but they both fell in with Brutus and Cassius when the assassins fled Rome and took control of Greece. The future poet and the politician's son fought on the losing side against the combined forces of Octavian and Antony in two battles at Philippi in October 42 BC. Cassius committed suicide thinking he'd lost the first encounter. Brutus followed suit when the armies met again. The republican cause of the old guard of Rome was finished.

There was nothing for Horace to do but slink back to Italy and his home in Venusia. He may be the town's most famous citizen now, praised everywhere and with that grand statue in the main square. But when he reached home after his unfortunate war he found his father's farm had been seized and handed over to an army veteran. Penniless and desperate he went to Rome where he escaped the threat of prosecution or worse under a general amnesty. He was a well-educated, bookish chap from his time in Greece, though looked down on by some since his father was a freedman, a former slave liberated by his master. Class always mattered to the Romans. One year after the amnesty, while working as a clerk in the Roman treasury, he was moving in arty circles in the city and met up with a fellow poet, Virgil. The two got on famously and soon Horace met Gaius Maecenas, a patron of the arts and one of Octavian's closest friends and advisers.

On the Esquiline Hill in Rome, not far from the unlovely park of Piazza Vittorio Emanuele, there's a diminutive brick building called the Auditorium of Maecenas. It's nothing to look at from the outside but if you manage to join one of the group visits – they need to be booked – you'll find a compact performance space, two thousand years old, complete with a few frescoes. This is all that remains of one of the most famous gardens of ancient Rome, the private paradise of Maecenas, a botanical wonder featuring flowers and trees from as far away as Persia.

Those meetings in the auditorium would sometimes be about politics, since for much of his life Maecenas was effectively the second-in-command to Octavian. But they'd also concern poetry and the arts. He loved the spoken word as much as he loved luxury and power, and soon became both friend and principal patron of Virgil and Horace, encouraging the young poets in their work. Horace didn't stay a clerk dealing with bureaucracy in the Roman treasury for long. Soon he was one of Maecenas's closest companions, and it's quite possible he and Virgil gave readings of their work in this small auditorium two thousand years ago.

As for those stories about the journey south... that was much more about politics than tourism. In 40 BC the triumvirate had signed the Treaty of Brundisium which gave Octavian the biggest prize, the western empire, to be run from Rome. Antony got the east, full of riches yet to be conquered, which he'd run from Alexandria where he'd taken Cleopatra, Caesar's former squeeze, as a lover. Lepidus, very much the junior partner and beginning to resent it, was confined to Africa.

Three years later the triumvirate met again at Tarentum to sign a new pact, one in which Maecenas played a key negotiating role. Horace's road trip may well have been an account of the journey to that vital meeting. It appears in his ten-poem book *Satires*. They were a sensation when they were published in Rome, establishing Horace's reputation as one of the city's finest poets alongside Virgil. A lot of scholarly thought has gone into decoding them, with the idea there's a deeper meaning that came from the delicate diplomatic mission he was embarked upon with Maecenas. The memory of war was recent. Horace, a spectator to its horrors and nearly a victim too, was perhaps subtly encouraging friendship as a way of settling the many differences between the two dominant forces in Roman politics, Octavian, now his master, and Antony. Not that he could come out and say it openly, since criticism of his boss in Rome, now twenty six, no longer a stripling, could still be dangerous.

Seven years later Horace had another book of poems for his fans, the first of his Odes. The thirty seventh of them was to contain a phrase that still resonates today... *Nunc est bibendum*. Now is the time to drink.

A jolly message you might think, and one Michelin adopted when it named the beaming tyre man Bibendum for its marketing and travel guides. But it isn't jolly at all. If the poems he wrote about his travels along the Via Appia with Maecenas were coded messages calling for amity among the rival partners in the Roman state, number thirty seven of the Odes shows he's very much picked sides. The work is about the defeat and death of Cleopatra at the end of the war that ensued once Lepidus was out of the way and Octavian and Antony were at each other's throats. Antony committed suicide as Octavian's forces entered Alexandria. Cleopatra did the same not long after, as countless books and films and TV shows have portrayed.

Our poet friend celebrated all this with verses for his master in which he describes the newly-dead Queen of Egypt as a *fatale monstrum*. A deadly monster if you like, though some say a subtler translation, such as a portent of doom, might be more appropriate. He then goes on to describe her suicide, grasping the poisonous viper to escape the ignominy of capture by Octavian.

> Amid her ruin'd halls she stood
> Unblench'd, and fearless to the end
> Grasp'd the fell snakes, that all her blood
> Might with the cold black venom blend,

> Death's purpose flushing in her face;
> Nor to our ships the glory gave,
> That she, no vulgar dame, should grace
> A triumph, crownless, and a slave.

Is this sympathy with the fallen woman? Or is he, as Roman writers often did, praising the defeated in order to make the victory of their patrons seem all the greater? Horace had now crossed the line. He was no longer an outsider from Venusia, slyly commenting on the complex politics of Rome, but a part of Octavian's court, a speech writer for him at times. An intellectual paid to praise the man who was now the undisputed leader of the Roman state.

On January 16, 27 BC, Plancus, the creep once buried in the mausoleum at Gaeta, proposed his change of name for the man born Gaius Octavius Thurinus. He was to be known as Augustus, self-styled *Imperator Caesar divi filius*. The Commander Caesar, son of a god. Plancus and Horace were, in the eyes of some, now paid sycophants to their patron. As Cicero feared when he tried to flee his executioners in Formia, the days of the republic were gone for good.

The King of Rome was back in all but name.

THE CITY MUSEUM in Brindisi is a delight, empty, free, with helpful staff pleased someone's come through the door. Roaming through room after room and floor after floor, every turning seems to reveal a fresh surprise. You don't have to look far to see who the main man was for Brundisium either. His likeness is everywhere, dug out of excavations, restored. In full military dress, decapitated so that all that's left is a barrel chest with ornate armour. Dressed as a priest with a toga over his head. Recovered from the sea too, since an entire section of the museum is dedicated to underwater archaeology.

This has been a busy, important port for more than two millennia, a gateway to and from the east. All along the coastline are ancient wrecks, sometimes visible at low tide, so many it's hard for the divers with their picks and baskets to keep up. A treasure trove of relics has been recovered over the years, some humble, some grand. Statues were obviously the must-have object for the rich of the day. Not just in Brindisi either. Throughout my trips up and down the Via Appia – in Taranto, Venosa, Benevento and all the smaller places further north – the same figure keeps popping up in civic museums. The Romans always loved to celebrate their famous men with statues. Augustus was going to be the most illustrious of the lot for all his long life. His wife Livia begins to appear too, severe, modest, maternal, seemingly the very opposite of the scheming, murderous woman she's so often painted in fiction.

After the turmoil of two centuries – Hannibal, Spartacus, the Social War, Sulla, the triumvirates – Rome finally finds a kind of peace under forty years of dictatorial rule. In order to seize the throne that had eluded those before him, Augustus was willing to lie and cheat, betray and murder any who stood in his way. Those stories about how he fought to keep Cicero's name off the proscription list, and later much regretted his death, I find a touch suspicious. He knew the old man he once called 'Father' was using him to defeat Antony, and would drop him, perhaps support his murder, once that was out of the way. Roman historians were always mindful of their own safety. The great Augustus was the father of the Roman Empire, not a name to be sullied by stories that suggested a vengeful nature. True, even in power, unassailable, he could put down plots and intrigue with instant cruelty, even turning on his own family from time to time. But that was politics. Business, not personal, to use the old gangster's phrase. As an individual, the hagiographers would have it, a great man would doubtless have flaws. But meanness and spite were usually deemed beneath them.

Besides, Rome had so many reasons to be grateful to the man once called Octavius who'd landed in Brundisium after Caesar's assassination, learning that he was the great soldier's chosen heir. As he boasted, he found the city of brick and left it a place of marble. The Rome we now associate with the imperial era began to appear during his reign: a city on the grandest of scales, magnificent to look at, in the centre at least, a formidable metropolis intent on establishing itself as the *caput mundi*, the capital of the world.

Under Augustus the empire would expand north to the Danube

and east to the Black Sea, seize the whole of the Iberian peninsula, Egypt and expand in Asia Minor. Where the military went, roads soon followed in the Via Appia's image, built by troops, maintained by a well-oiled bureaucracy. Augustus knew how important infrastructure was to the growing Roman state and restructured the administration to deal with the roads to the provinces. According to one historian he took on the job of roads superintendent himself for a while. The importance of road building to the empire is clear from the narrative told on Trajan's Column, the towering monument in Rome dedicated to the emperor's campaign to subdue modern Romania. Alongside scenes of battle, victory and domination there are frequent carvings of soldiers chopping down trees and laying the foundation of the roads that would lead them to the enemy.

In France, Augustus's favourite general, Agrippa, oversaw the creation of a new network of highways running out from the hub of Lugdunum (Lyon) in all four directions through Gaul. The route that took his name, the Via Agrippa, finally stretched from Arelate (Arles) all the way to Colonia (Cologne). In Spain the Via Augusta ran for 930 miles from Gades (Cádiz), inland to Hispalis (Seville), then north along the coast and to Narbo (Narbonne), forming the principal main route from Spain to Italy. As in Italy, the routes the roads took often form the basis of today's motorways. Sections of the N340 coastal highway from Cádiz to Barcelona not only follow the same path but, until the road was modernised in the early part of the twentieth century, used the original cobbled surface too.

Under Augustus, the empire became larger, more affluent, prouder and yet more arrogant, enriched by architecture and literature, much of it pinched from Greece, populated by a teeming class of workers and slaves at the foot of society, and a small, highly privileged aristocracy that flitted between the great cities of Europe and their palatial villas on the coast as easily as wealthy travellers of today fly to New York for the weekend.

Once such a starchy guardian of its own identity, unwilling even to share its citizenship with its neighbours until forced, it was now becoming international, multi-racial, filled with cultures from other nations that had been absorbed into the body of the Roman state.

Which would inevitably raise the question... when society, at all levels, high and low, became home to people who spoke different languages and followed other gods, what did it mean to be Roman anymore?

~

As if to hammer home the point that some things never change, Rome had its fair share of old-fashioned so-called traditionalists forever bleating, 'Them Egyptians, them Jews, coming over here with all their funny clothes and food and ideas. What happened to the good old days, eh? Why can't we go back to being just us without all this foreign vermin?'

You even get a bit of that in literature when poets such as Virgil and Horace write wistfully of an Arcadia lost in what they regard as a fallen modern world. This kind of phoney supposed nationalism was as ill-placed then as it is now. The golden age they harked back to never existed. The Rome without ambition, before Appius Claudius Caecus began building his road south to Capua, was a place of mud huts, poverty and middling importance in a divided Italy. The new world of Augustus, complex and multi-faceted, depended on other races – for trade, for slavery, for entertainment in the arenas and theatres, more and more in the growing armies demanding fresh troops to fill their ranks. A few intellectuals may have hated the perceived threat to Rome's moral purity from all these alien outsiders. But the average citizen loved so many of the things they brought with them.

One of the abiding characteristics of Roman society, high and low, was its boundless inquisitiveness, a curiosity about the fast-changing, fluid world it inhabited. There was a deep and almost childlike love of the new, whether it was a religious cult, a fashion, some kind of food or a different sort of furniture or decoration. In Pompeii the walls of one of the richer villas was found to be decorated with frescoes not of beautiful Campania but Egypt, complete with hippos and crocodiles. Augustus received ambassadors from far beyond the Mediterranean and Asia Minor where he ruled. India and China, states along the Silk Road, all came to call. They left strange spices and ceramics, and took back goods in return. Roman glassware from the first century BC has been excavated in Guangzhou in southern China and found in Afghanistan. In the Naples Archaeological Museum there's a fresco from Pompeii that shows a nymph wearing a distinctly flimsy silk dress, doubtless made from imported Chinese fabric. It was a fashion so common among the upper classes that the cantankerous philosopher Seneca the Elder howled against such an assault on common decency on the grounds that 'the woman's husband is no more familiar with her body than any passing stranger'.

And there's the problem for the traditionalists. However much they might rail against the degradation of traditional Roman values, people didn't just like the foreign and the exotic. They loved them. There's an illustration of the changes happening throughout the growing empire to be found underground in what was once Capua.

FOR YEARS the place was closed to the public. Now you pay a pittance at the ticket desk of the amphitheatre, have a drink or a bite to eat in the organic cafe admiring the view, and wait for a friendly guide to arrive. Then it's a walk through the back streets until you stop at a metal door in a shabby little alley called Vico Mitreo.

The clue is in the name. Here's a mithraeum, a very unusual temple to a very unusual god, Mithras. You can find mithraeums all over the territory of the Roman empire. There's one in a field in the far north of England on Hadrian's Wall. Another was famously discovered in the City of London and is now a free site to visit in the footings of the headquarters of the Bloomberg financial empire. Hungary and Bosnia, Syria and a number of sites in Germany all boast remains. But Capua's is one of the finest, not that you realise as you descend the modern steps into the dark cavern below.

When the lights come on you see it: a subterranean meeting room for the followers of the Mithras cult, an underground chamber beneath a barrel-vault ceiling, with benches on both sides and at the end the high point, the altar complete with the required fresco. This is a cult that is still only loosely understood and looking at the painting in Capua it's not hard to see why. The god Mithras is depicted sacrificing a white bull, stabbing a dagger into the animal's chest, an act known as the 'tauroctony'. A dog and a serpent reach for the spurting blood.

The followers of the cult were often from the military, and in Capua, home to such a famous gladiator school, could well have included the masters of that too. They had to go through a seven-part initiation before being allowed to know some of its secrets. Feasting and perhaps business talk were probably part of the process too – a kind of Roman freemasonry if you like.

From the number of mithraeums found throughout Europe and beyond it's clear this was a very popular brotherhood. But it certainly wasn't Roman. It's not even European, like most of the other gods Rome imported. Mithraism originated in Persia and began to be adopted then developed by the Romans around the time of Augustus. All that trade from the east through Brundisium and elsewhere didn't just deliver silk and spice and slaves. It brought culture, and the Romans lapped it up. The empire they were creating had started coming home. Just as Victorian England found itself entranced by the Raj in India, and Queen Victoria acquired an Indian servant, Abdul Karim, the Munshi, as one of her closest attendants, the high society of Rome came to love the exotic and the strange from their colonies. While those lower down the ladder grew up in a world where travel, across great distances, to lands quite foreign to them, was part of everyday life.

The military, too, was now a mix of races from all over the empire, with different languages and different gods. A legionary from Ethiopia once surprised the emperor Septimius Severus on Hadrian's Wall by presenting him with a garland. The emperor was unamused – black was the colour of death for the Romans and he took it as a bad omen. At least he escaped with his life. According to the historian Appian, a black soldier in Brutus's forces at Philippi was hacked to death by his comrades who took the colour of his skin as a bad omen before the battle.

The soldiers who patrolled Britain on behalf of Rome included men from modern Iraq, Croatia, Belgium and the Netherlands. Septimius Severus himself was no Roman. He was born in Libya and came from a family that was originally Carthaginian. His empress Julia Domna came from Emesa (Homs) in Syria.

While Rome was sending armies down the Via Appia to embark east for conquest and domination, floods of people from the outposts of empire, traders, would-be soldiers, wheeler-dealers, physicians, fortune-tellers and cranks were flooding up the road in the other direction, attracted by the wealth and dynamism of the great *caput mundi*. Those soldiers and business figures wining and dining in Capua's underground mithraeum while they went through the secret rituals of a religion pinched from distant Persia would have been as cosmopolitan as their peers in similar Mithraic caverns being built throughout the empire. Bearers of the badge of Rome, aware that they were under the thumb of whoever ruled in the capital, though many might never see the city at all. The long peace that Augustus brought didn't just turn brick to marble around the Forum and the Capitol Hill. It began a slow and irreversible shift in what it meant to be 'Roman', one that ill-tempered traditionalists saw as a threat to the city itself. In the words of Tacitus, 'It was thus an altered world, and of the old, unspoilt Roman character not a trace lingered.'

＄ 14 ＄

EVEN GODS DIE

WHILE HE WAS ALIVE, Augustus allowed himself to be hailed as divine
by fawning cities in the distant reaches of the empire. Being foreigners, they were thought to know no better. Rome, however, would never
countenance the idea of a living god. There were even those who
hoped that, once he was gone, the republic of old might be reborn.
The question of succession would not go away.

He had no son of his own, but, like Caesar before him, an adopted
heir for a while, Agrippa Postumus, his grandson. But his wife, Livia,
had a son through her first marriage, Tiberius, and as Augustus grew
older he seemed a more suitable choice. Postumus, a violent, aggressive individual, was banished to a tiny island, Planasia (Planosa) off the
Tuscan coast in strange circumstances.

In the summer of AD 14, as his health was failing, the seventy-five-
year-old Augustus was due to accompany Tiberius to Beneventum to
see him off on the journey to Brundisium and a campaign across the
Adriatic. Instead, he cancelled and was rumoured to have made a
mysterious journey to see the exiled Postumus. After that he sailed
first to Capreae (Capri) then Neapolis before, growing ever weaker, he
travelled to his father's old house in Nola. There he was met by
Tiberius who'd turned back from the east after receiving a letter from

his mother. Livia joined them. Aware he was dying, Augustus looked at those around him and said, '*Acta est fabula, plaudite.* The play is over, applaud.'

On August the nineteenth he died, peacefully, unlike most of the men he'd fought with over the years. His body was taken back in solemn convoys first to Capua, then along the Via Appia. Magistrates from the local towns carried his bier, moving by night because of the heat, staying in temples, travelling past mourning crowds lining the road. The father of the nation was dead. No one knew what came next. On the start of that last flat long stretch at Bovilllae, the equestrian order of Rome rode out to carry his bier into the city.

The funeral pyre was built in the Campus Martius, and his remains interred in the circular mausoleum he'd built for himself close to the Tiber. It's still there, a rather sad ruin currently being restored, closed and somewhat behind schedule. Next to it, however, is the wonderful Ara Pacis, the altar of peace the Senate erected in the Campus Martius five years before his death. It's a glorious piece of propaganda for the Augustan age, a celebration of history, from the tale of Romulus and Remus, to conquests of foreign nations and a series of portraits of stately Roman senators. A sign of how much he was loved. Or feared. Or both.

But was he murdered too? The gossip – so beautifully used by Robert Graves in *I, Claudius* – was that Augustus had realised Postumus had been framed for the offence that saw him banished. He'd gone to Planasia for a reconciliation that would lead to his grandson's return to Rome and restoration as Augustus's preferred heir. Livia, determined that her son, Tiberius, would wear the crown poisoned her husband using the figs he loved to eat from the garden in Nola. Then she arranged for Postumus to be put to the sword by a guard in his island jail so that Augustus's plan could be taken no further.

Roman gossip or a real-life murder mystery? Postumus was certainly killed after Augustus died, though he hardly seems to have been the admirable character Graves paints. And Tiberius did, with bribes and pressure, become the next Emperor of Rome for twenty two years.

Rumours of poison, murder plots and even witchcraft abounded in Roman society. Some were doubtless based on fact, others nothing more than a lack of medical understanding and gossip, idle or malicious. Most of us would think it a stretch to accuse a wife of murdering her husband of fifty years. Though perhaps, as a few have suggested, she was helping Augustus die an easier death by supplying some kind of drug. He had been ill for some time and close to the brink on several occasions before. Or else it's just the product of a feverish, overly dramatic historian's imagination. It wouldn't be the first time, or the last.

Anyone following Augustus, the father of Rome, onto the throne would have found themselves in his shadow. Tiberius, a surly, private, misanthropic fellow, seems to have felt that way even before he inherited the job. The empire continued to expand almost by the momentum of its size and bureaucratic and military efficiency. But the richer Rome became, the more Tiberius seemed to hate the place and the role he found himself in. Surrounded by plots, a bickering family, and a Senate that loathed him, he fumed and feuded and soon became a byword for cruelty.

Suetonius wrote...

Not a day passed without an execution, not even those that were sacred and holy; for he put some to death even on New Year's day. Many were accused and condemned with their children and even by their children. The relatives of the victims were forbidden to mourn for them. Special rewards were voted the accusers and sometimes even the witnesses. The word of no informer was doubted. Every crime was treated as capital, even the utterance of a few simple words. A poet was charged with having slandered Agamemnon in a tragedy, and a writer of history of having called Brutus and Cassius the last of the Romans. The writers were at once put to death and their works destroyed, although they had been read with approval in public some years before in the presence of Augustus himself.

After eleven years of increasingly embittered political life in the capital, Tiberius abandoned the city for a seemingly squalid idyll of debauchery, engaging in sexual depravity with children, embarking on murderous campaigns against any that crossed him. And all in the most beautiful of surroundings, the Villa Jovis on Capreae, the ruins of which you can still visit today, a long and beautiful walk up from the glitzy, star-struck town below.

It's one of the more charming sights on Capri, an island ruined by money in many parts. As you take the meandering path up from the town, gardens and vegetable plots begin to appear as it turns into the Via Tiberio. Handsome goats flock over the ruins of the Villa Jovis – perhaps as a nod to the theory that the island's name comes from them. In one local's garden there's a roughshod outdoor cafe where a beer won't cost you an arm and a leg and the cheery owner will make you a panino from the tomatoes in his plot. The remains of the palace are atmospheric rather than stunning. But if you've read any of the stories about the old beast, especially by Graves, you may get a shiver seeing the spot where Tiberius was frightened out of his wits by a fisherman who emerged with his catch, a large lobster, as a present, then ordered the man thrown off the cliffs, but only after his spiny gift was rubbed in the poor chap's face.

The running of the empire was left first to Sejanus, a corrupt and bloodthirsty officer of the Praetorian Guard, whose execution was ordered by Tiberius from Capreae when he was suspected of seizing power for himself. After that his place was taken by an equally ruthless member of the guard, Macro. Twice Tiberius almost came back to the city, once by boat, another time reaching the seven-mile marker of the Via Appia before seeing the city walls and turning back.

In March 37 AD, he decided to return one last time. He had only reached the shore at Misenum (Miseno) when he was taken ill. And here the gossips return. With him at the time was Caligula, his nephew, and the guard Macro. One night in bed Tiberius appeared to stop breathing. Caligula seized the imperial ring from his finger and was about to announce the emperor was dead and he was now in charge. Then Tiberius woke and began to wonder what was going on. At this point Caligula or Macro, or perhaps both, smothered him.

So hated was the old man that, when his bier reached Rome, the mobs who'd wept at Augustus's death demanded his corpse be thrown into the Tiber like that of a common criminal. Instead, he was swiftly cremated and his ashes placed alongside those of Augustus.

Were the first two emperors of Rome really murdered? We'll never know. But if the historians weren't simply passing on sensationalist tittle-tattle then both Augustus and Tiberius died in what the police would call 'domestics'. Family disputes, albeit ones that happened at the very pinnacle of the Roman state.

Caligula was headed for a much grimmer end, one that would set the tone for all who occupied the imperial throne after him. A short trip from Rome along the Via Appia into the quiet, wooded beauty of the Alban Hills reveals why.

IV
DECLINE AND FALL

Nemi in the Alban hills, home to Caligula's pleasure craft.

$$
\text{\Large ❧ } \textit{15} \text{ \Large ❧}
$$

THE PRIEST IN THE HILLS

CLOSE TO WHAT was once Bovillae, where Milo and Clodius fought and Rome's knights came to carry Augustus's bier, the old road vanishes beneath its modern counterpart, the Via Appia Nuova. This hectic highway winds its way into the Alban Hills, commuter territory for those working in Rome but wanting somewhere quieter and cheaper to live. Tourists generally aim for Castel Gandolfo and the site of the Pope's summer palace. Food lovers head for Ariccia and *porchetta*. The Appia Antica reappears at Albano where it's a narrow country lane, often in poor repair, running past vineyards, small farms and rural homes. Driving here is a challenge for the bravest of motorists only. Best to stick to the main road then, after Ariccia, take a left turn towards Nemi, a mountain village with quite a tale to tell.

A good way to appreciate the extraordinary geography of the Alban Hills is to open a satellite map, or the Google Earth Project that accompanies this book, and view them from above. There you'll see two near identical lakes, Albano and Nemi, perfect circles of dark blue set amidst thickly forested hills. It's hard for the geologically ignorant like me to understand that this verdant green paradise is actually the product of volcanic activity. Or, as the Smithsonian puts it, 'a large Pleistocene stratovolcano... formed during an eruptive period with six major explosive eruptions that produced at least 280 square kilometres of ejecta between about 560,000 and 350,000 years ago'.

There's still seismic activity around here from time to time, and carbon dioxide leaks that have killed livestock. That only adds to the remote, mystical air of the place. It's hard to believe Rome is just a thirty-minute train ride from Ariccia. Travelling between the two feels more like going from London all the way to distant Cornwall.

Long before there were cities of any kind in Italy, this was an area populated by hill tribes, drawn by the rich farmland on the slopes and the idea that somewhere so strange and beautiful had to be home to the gods. Monte Cavo, the peak to the east of the lakes, was a holy mountain to the Italic people who first lived here. The Romans built a temple to Jove on the summit. Each spring the ruling consuls would lead a festival to celebrate the founding of the city and pray for its continued prosperity. They'd walk there in procession, on a sacred path from the Via Appia in Ariccia, to sacrifice in honour of military victories too.

Anywhere this beautiful is going to attract the wealthy looking for another estate to add to their portfolio. It wasn't just emperors who loved to build their palaces and villas on the slopes around Albano and Nemi. The aristocratic rich wanted their piece of the land too. A place by the sea, around Formia or in the Bay of Naples, was essential. But the lovely shoreline of Campania was days away. From Rome, in a baking summer, you could be in the cool heights of the Alban Hills in a day, carried in a guarded litter along the Via Appia. Trying to follow in their footsteps along what was once the sacred path is no longer so enchanting. Now Monte Cavo is a military installation, the summit covered with ugly buildings and antennae, all barred to the public. Never mind. There are still plenty of beautiful walks to be had if you pick up the local tourist information provided by the Regional Park of the Castelli Romani.

Those two lakes are calderas, super-craters formed by a volcano collapsing in upon itself. They're not so deep but extraordinarily beautiful, like dazzling sapphire jewels set in the green necklace of the hills. On the shore of Nemi there was a sacred grove and a temple dedicated to Diana Nemorensis, Diana of Nemi, a deity related to the Greek

Artemis. If you choose the time right, close to a full moon with clear skies, you can view the whole lake from the village on the hill above and realise why it's still known as *Lo Specchio di Diana*, the mirror of Diana. And why the locals held this mountain paradise in such awe.

The temple of Diana was under the control of a priest known as the *Rex Nemorensis*, king of the grove. Since the cult of Diana seemed to have some distant connection to human sacrifice, the chap was chosen in a very unusual way – by mortal combat. He could only be replaced by a runaway slave who found his way to Nemi, plucked a bough from the sacred oak there, then challenged the incumbent to a fight to the death. This is the ritual recorded by James Frazier in *The Golden Bough*. It was also the inspiration for poets, among them Ovid who wrote (in a translation by Macaulay)...

> From the still glassy lake that sleeps
> Beneath Aricia's trees–
> Those trees in whose dim shadow
> The ghastly priest doth reign,
> The priest who slew the slayer,
> And shall himself be slain.

The tradition was also recorded by the historian Strabo, who wrote of the terror it instilled in the winner...

> *...a barbaric... element predominates in the sacred usages, for the people set up as priest merely a run-away slave who has slain with his own hand the man previously consecrated to that office; accordingly the priest is always armed with a sword, looking around for the attacks, and ready to defend himself. The temple is in a sacred grove, and in front of it is a lake which resembles an open sea, and round about it in a circle lies an unbroken and very high mountain-brow, which encloses both the temple and the water in a place that is hollow and deep.*

Which is pretty much the scene today though the temple with its golden roof is long gone leaving just a collection of ruins on a farm with no easy access. One of the most impressive artefacts to survive from the Nemi temple belongs to the British Museum, a half life-size statue of a priestess or goddess, a young woman in an elegant *chiton* tunic, high girdle and mantle, with a torc neck ring and bracelets round her outstretched arms.

Death and renewal. Gladiatorial combat. And a sacred grove where every August women would come from Rome bearing torches and gifts as offerings to the cult. With a story like that it's not hard to imagine Nemi was quite the destination for everyone who could make the trip.

And emperors too.

THERE ARE lots of stories about Caligula. How he planned to make his horse Consul and order the toffs of Rome to come and dine in the beast's glorious home. The time he threw some unfortunate folk in the audience into the arena to be devoured by lions because the event had run out of slaves. There was the bridge he built across part of the Bay of Naples, designed to look like the Via Appia, just so that he could ride across it first on horseback then in a chariot. As for the countless murders, the incest, the robberies, the rapes and the erotic singing and dancing...

We'll leave it there. From Robert Graves to the movie directed by the Italian soft porn director Tinto Brass and scripted, sort of, by Gore Vidal, Caligula's more than colourful life has been played out in print and on screen time and time again. How many of those stories are true? Given the number you'd think quite a few. But that tale about his horse being lined up to be Consul may just come from him cracking a joke – the horse was never given that rank. *Storia.* History or story. Often it's hard to tell.

One thing we know for sure. Caligula adored the wild green hills around Nemi. Since he regarded himself as a god too, perhaps he thought he was, for once, in the company of his peers. What he didn't like was the slow turnover in the role of that unfortunate priest, the Nemorensis king. According to Suetonius, the increasingly unstable emperor became so bored with the fact the same chap had been in Diana's temple for years that he hired an adversary to attack him. The outcome isn't recorded, but it's hard to imagine Caligula would have tolerated his man losing.

He'd have known the area around Nemi of old since it was one of the most popular resorts for the Roman rich looking for a country pad in the Alban Hills. Caesar owned a palatial villa by the water. Cicero had been summoned there for a private chat with Brutus just two months after his assassination. Caligula, ever intent on outdoing them all, decided to go one better and build his palace *on* the sacred lake itself. It came in the form of two, perhaps three, huge boats, not the kind of thing you'd take to sea, but more like floating mansions with turrets, brick lodgings, baths and dining areas, the hulls hewn from wood cut down from the neighbouring forests. He loved his ships, and presumably the Nemi ones followed the design of his coastal vessels described by Suetonius, 'ten banks of oars, with sterns set with gems, multi-coloured sails, huge spacious baths, colonnades, and banquet-halls, and even a great variety of vines and fruit trees so that, on board, he might recline at table from an early hour'.

Ridiculously expensive and extravagant follies fit for a ridiculously expensive and extravagant emperor. For once we know this odd story really is true. For centuries the gigantic hulls of Caligula's strange fleet sat beneath the crystal waters of Lake Nemi taunting everyone who saw them there. What gold and treasure might be found if only they could be explored or, even better, brought to the surface?

In the fifteenth and sixteenth centuries recovery attempts were made with lifting gear and a primitive diving suit, but all they managed to retrieve was wood, brick ruins and a few nails. Then, at the end of the nineteenth century, a more scientific and organised inspection of the lake began. It found two vessels lying on the bed, one sixty four metres long and twenty wide, the second seventy one metres long and twenty four wide. Still, no one could work out how to raise them from the bottom. Then an engineer came up with a bright and original idea: instead of bringing the boats to the surface, why not take the surface down to the boats?

In 1928, at the prompting of Mussolini, the lake was drained in an expensive and technically quite astonishing piece of engineering. One discovery that helped was an ancient channel, dating back to pre-

Roman times which was used to supply water to surrounding areas. It's still there, well-hidden in the greenery by Nemi's edge, first built more than two and a half millennia ago.

After much expensive pumping and a few collapses in the lake bed, the hulls and what contents they still had were revealed and, slowly, hauled to shore. There was little in the way of treasure – perhaps they'd been looted before being sunk. But some bronze fitments, among them a stunning head of Medusa, can now be found in the Palazzo Massimo alle Terme, the national museum in Rome. What was obvious from the wrecks, however, was the indulgent scale of Caligula's pleasure ships. There was evidence of buildings, staircases and places for banks of rowers, even though Nemi's scarcely much of a lake to cross. Pumps fed hot water for baths and cold for fountains. A complex pulley and turntable process provided a way of getting heavy objects onto the boat. All in all, the size and construction of the vessels proved the Romans were far more technologically advanced than many historians had suspected.

This delighted Mussolini, a chap who modelled himself on the emperors of old and loved the idea of rebuilding at least part of the original Roman Empire. He chose as the emblem of his Fascist Party the *fasces,* the bundles of rods that *lictors,* bodyguards and general enforcers for the state, carried in imperial times.

Hitler soon copied this idea and, being Hitler, did everything bigger. The standards the Nazis carried were based on those of Roman centurions. The marching area he built at Nuremberg was called the Märzfeld after the Campus Martius, the military field in the centre of Rome. Even the Nazi salute – *Heil Hitler* – was based upon the way emperors were greeted – *Ave Caesar*.

All the hallmarks that would later define modern fascism – the rule of force and the military, colonisation and rigidly enforced imperialism, the subjugation of individual freedoms in deference to the control of an almighty state – weren't just present in the Roman Empire as it spread its eagle wings across Europe and beyond. They were critical elements of it, foundation stones that underpinned the way Rome worked.

Mussolini saw all those statues of Augustus and his successors, the once-magnificent buildings of the Forum and beyond, and wanted to leave his mark too. As an heir to the Caesars, he demanded his monuments. One was to be a museum built by the lakeside to house the gigantic, reconstructed hulls of Caligula's mad pleasure craft. The building's still there, probably close to the site of Caesar's old villa, and has the recognisably brutalist modern design of so much architecture from the Fascist era, oddly juxtaposed against the secluded beauty of its surroundings. The place was so deserted when I turned up that, just as at Minturnae, I had to search for someone to sell me a ticket. The original wooden structures were lost in the Second World War during a firefight between German soldiers who'd occupied the museum and an attacking American force. But there are replicas of bits of the originals, along with some statuary and historical background about the temple of Diana sitting in a farm field around the corner. The parts that are left are impressive but seem out of scale with the massive building where they're displayed. The reason is simple: they're one fifth size copies of fragments of the vessels that came out of the water, models built in the navy shipyards in Naples. The originals would have filled this massive, hangar-like building.

Historical photographs show they were simply huge, as does some contemporary news footage from Pathé you'll find on YouTube. They were also ridiculous indulgences, with no purpose except to massage the ego of a dictator in love with himself. Recent explorations have suggested there may be yet another of Caligula's boats lying on the lake bed, perhaps two. Though given the cost of recovery, it seems unlikely they will come to light for a while, if ever.

THE MUSEUM IS a pleasant walk from the village of Nemi on the hill above, or a leisurely drive around the lake. Today the area is best known for the micro-climate that produces crops of wild strawberries. Each year a festival dedicated to the delicious little fruit brings thousands into Nemi. Grab an outside seat with a wonderful view over the lake at the Bar delle Fragole and you can enjoy an *aperitivo della casa*, sparkling wine with a crush of tiny strawberries, a kind of Bellini of the

Alban Hills. Even better if it's a moonlit summer night and that silver disc is shining back at you from Diana's mirror below. Caligula is still remembered hereabouts. There's a wine named after him, very appropriately if the stories are correct, and a small poster on the wall when I visited told me I'd just missed a local festival to mark his birthday, August the thirty first. Just food and drink, one assumes, not live re-enactments.

Augustus, the first emperor, may have come to power through blood and treachery, but he later mellowed and was genuinely mourned by many as the father of the empire when he died. Tiberius, an odd, anti-social character, was loathed and loathed back in return, bloodily after a while. Caligula snatched the imperial wreath before anyone could stop him. Perhaps even before Tiberius had breathed his last, all with the help of a well-paid military. What the ridiculous folly of the ships of Nemi confirms is that once in power he soon moved on from run-of-the-mill dictatorship to overweening, selfish tyranny. While he threw money at his profligate pleasure barges in the Alban Hills, he was busily pillaging the population and his enemies, killing them and stealing their wealth and their property for no other reason than he needed the money to pay for the lifestyle he thought fitting of a god.

It was hardly a surprise that those around him began to hate his relentless terror. How much they were appalled by his behaviour and how much they simply wondered when the lunatic might turn on them, it's impossible to judge. If Augustus and Tiberius genuinely were the victims of domestic murders, Caligula would bring a new brand of regicide to Rome. In January 41 AD he was walking along a tunnel in the palace complex on the Palatine – the Neronian Cryptoporticus probably, somewhere in the palace known as the Domus Tiberiana which now mostly sits beneath the Farnese Gardens. A narrow, damp underground passageway where the emperor of the known world would breath his last. His own guards stabbed him to death then entered the imperial palaces and murdered his wife and one-year-old daughter. For a moment the fate of Rome hung in the balance as the Senate gathered and tried to cobble together some means of restoring the republic. Before they could agree a thing, the Praetorians decided an emperor was a better bet and placed Claudius, Caligula's uncle, on the throne. The imperial line was resumed.

Robert Graves tells the story beautifully, much of it based on the histories of Tacitus and others. His Claudius is a genial intellectual, posing as a bumbling clown in order to survive the desperate times, forced onto the throne against his will. A republican at heart, he wants to bring the age of the emperors to an end. But that always eludes him as he becomes the creature he hates most, a monster, trapped in dictatorial rule. It's a great *storia*, definitely a story not history. In truth, Claudius could be as ruthless and bloodthirsty as his predecessors, though mostly without the extravagance and histrionics.

Caligula's end changed the terms of the job. It was no longer hereditary, that of a monarch, respected and obeyed for life. The imperial garland rested on the support of the military and the political class around the Senate. There would be more than sixty emperors of Rome over the next three centuries. At most, seventeen can be said to have died of natural causes for sure.

Any man who rose to the ultimate position would know that one day he might be challenged for the throne – and either kill defending it or die himself. Caligula had brought the reign of the Rex Nemorensis to an early end out of nothing more than boredom. But from his rule onwards every Roman emperor was, in effect, a new Rex Nemorensis, wondering who the next plotter might be, whether close family, or distant, a general in the provinces with an army at his back, or simply a disgruntled slave or servant looking for revenge.

❧ 16 ☙

THE RICH GROW EVER RICHER

CALIGULA'S vanished ships in Nemi offer a tantalising glimpse of the excesses of the upper classes of Roman society. For something grander and more tangible, let's head back to the coast and turn the time machine back a few years to the rule of Tiberius. Sperlonga is a handsome seaside town between Terracina and Gaeta, just off the Via Appia. There's a beach, a small harbour and all the usual cafes and restaurants you'd expect in a tiny, very Italian resort. Its name comes from the Latin 'spelunca' meaning cave – the source of the American term 'spelunking' for exploring underground. On the edge of the town, you find out why.

The place I was looking for stands to the east, at the foot of a small hill, the Monte Ciannito, just before the road tunnel beneath it. It's easily missed, and the parking's not obvious, though you could walk the mile or so along the beach if you have the time. From the road all you see are some railings and a sign 'Museo Archeologico Nazionale Antro di Tiberio' with a low modern building behind. 'Antro' means cave, and this is quite a cave indeed.

Today's museum is the modern entrance to the villa built for Tiberius two thousand years ago. Grouch that he was, he still felt excess and luxury were his imperial right wherever he happened to lay his head. Sperlonga was probably an overnight stop on the way to his favourite palaces in Capraea.

There's not a lot left of his original complex except an expanse of walls that shows it was quite some size as it sprawled down the low hill towards the shore. One curiosity is that there are still fish ponds, features that were popular with all villa owners, for food and amusement. Today they're home to fat grey mullet, though Tiberius probably had more exotic fare around.

Across the gulf, just round the corner in the Bay of Naples, past the island of Nisida where Brutus plotted to kill Caesar, sit the remains of the villa of an unpleasant businessman called Vedius Pollio in what's now the archaeological park of Pausilypon. He was a pal of Augustus, and raised a temple to him – long lost –in Beneventum. Vedius was fond of treating his slaves with great cruelty but very considerate towards the lampreys he kept in pools at the villa shoreline. If a slave offended him, he threw the unfortunate into the water to be devoured by the fish. Once, when Augustus was visiting, a servant broke a valuable goblet and was about to be fed to the lampreys when he fell to his knees and begged the emperor for mercy. The offended Augustus freed him, then ordered all of Vedius's glasses to be smashed and his precious pools filled in.

There's no record of man-eating lampreys at Sperlonga, though that doesn't mean they were never there. Beyond the ponds, however, sits the star attraction, the grotto of Tiberius, rediscovered in the 1950s, with the astonishing findings inside now recreated in the museum up the hill.

Sperlonga is one of several places along this stretch of coast that claims links with the Greek hero Odysseus. Supposedly, he landed in the area on his long and circuitous journey home after the Trojan Wars. Tiberius seems to have been a fan of the Greek hero, and felt this relationship should be recorded in the pleasure grotto he had built in the natural cave beneath the hill. You can see the scale and ambition of the statues that once filled the grotto from the remains in the modern museum. One set depicts the blinding of Polyphemus, the vast, drunk, cyclops about to have his lone eye poked out by Odysseus holding a stake. Another, which would have sat in the middle of the pool that's still there today, shows his ship being attacked by the sea monster Scylla.

They were in pieces when the grotto was uncovered in the 1950s, and it's fair to say a touch of creativity has gone into putting them back together with some new casts to fill in the holes. It's a stunning spot all the same and you can only imagine the awe felt by the simple fishermen in the hamlet of Sperlonga at having the ruler of the world enjoying parties around the corner. Given the vile stories told about his habits at his villa in Capreae, we can only wonder, too, what went on here, in his solitary cavern, surrounded by images of his mythical hero. Those dank, algae-slimed walls doubtless have some tales to tell.

One we know for fact. Around 26 AD, with Tiberius already sick of Rome and determined to spend as much time outside the city as possible, he was dining in the grotto when the ceiling collapsed.

Both Suetonius and Tacitus record what happened, Tacitus saying...

The rocks at its entrance suddenly fell in and crushed some of the attendants; thereupon panic seized the whole company and there was a general flight of the guests. Sejanus hung over the emperor, and with knee, face, and hand encountered the falling stones; and was found in this attitude by the soldiers who came to their rescue. After this he was greater than ever and, though his counsels were ruinous, he was listened to with confidence, as a man who had no care for himself.

The historian adds that the event gave Tiberius 'grounds for trusting more fully in the friendship and fidelity of Sejanus' for saving his life. It only took another five years for him to decide his saviour was getting too big for his boots in Rome and have him killed. Tiberius was never big on trust.

THE BODY COUNT surrounding the imperial throne after Caligula is quite staggering. Two more emperors related to the family of Augustus followed, Claudius then Nero. Claudius may have been poisoned at

Nero's instigation. Nero committed suicide when faced with execution after the Senate decided he was an enemy of the state.

After that, the job of emperor truly was in the realm of that priest by the lake in Nemi. In 69 AD alone there were four emperors, the first three either murdered or committing suicide. The next dynasty along, the Flavians, lasted for just three incumbents.

There were 'good emperors' among the mediocre and the downright bad. Hadrian (ruled 117 AD to 138 AD) always gets a favourable press for his love of architecture and his realisation that the empire was too large to control and needed to shrink rather than expand. Marcus Aurelius (emperor or co-emperor from 161 AD to 180 AD), the philosopher king whose meditations still prove a bestseller, is perhaps an early example of what today would be called 'woke', someone in touch with spirituality and morality while trying to handle the day job of running an empire. But then he picked his son Commodus as heir, a disastrous choice. The movie *Gladiator* really did get the character of Commodus spot on. He enjoyed fighting in the arena, and naturally always won. But he didn't die there. He was poisoned and strangled in his bath by his wrestling partner.

This was the cue, not for the return of republican Rome as the film suggested, but a year in which five individuals claimed the imperial crown, one of whom had simply bought it from the Praetorian guard. You didn't even need to be a true-born Roman any more. Hadrian grew up in Spain, where his family had lived for more than two hundred years, and only got the job through a slightly dodgy act of adoption.

Some of the emperors who followed were a waste of a good toga. Men like Aemilianus, a Libyan or Moor from north Africa who held down the job for twelve weeks or so in 253 AD before being murdered by his own troops. Eutropius, a historian writing a century later, summed him up, 'Aemilianus came from an extremely insignificant family, his reign was even more insignificant, and he was slain in the third month.' And there you have it.

A good many others proved the point that being a homicidal fruitcake was no obstacle provided you had the money and military support. In 217 AD the army fell behind Macrinus, a Berber from North Africa, when his predecessor, Caracalla, was stabbed to death while relieving himself at the side of the road in Turkey. One year after becoming emperor Macrinus was killed after his opponents paid to place a fourteen-year-old Syrian called Elagabalus on the throne. The kid married five times – once to a Vestal Virgin which was, as the name suggests, somewhat against the rules – and later to a male athlete he came to like. The Praetorian Guard hired to protect him decapitated the lad along with his mother and threw their naked bodies into the Tiber when he was just eighteen.

By the fourth century power was being shared across east and west between individuals who were frequently at odds with one another and with the Senate, clinging to power through money and military might alone.

The ground was shifting beneath their feet.

❧   17   ❦

BACK TO THE ETERNAL CITY

THE WEATHER WAS TURNING by the time I got back to Rome. Spots of rain speckled the dusty windscreen, autumn whispering its imminent arrival. I dropped off the Abarth at Fiumicino and told the woman on the rental desk what a wonderful car I thought it was. She laughed and said, 'Everyone tells me that – it's why we get so many stolen. Did you know if that had happened we'd have put three thousand euros on your credit card?'

No, I didn't. That would have made my night in the rough end of Taranto's Old Town, with the little beast parked outside in a distinctly worse for wear street, a touch more nerve-racking. The Via Appia may be three hundred and fifty miles long but I'd covered four times that distance driving from Rome to Brindisi and back, ticking off sights along the way. Now I needed one more look at that stretch of road closest to Rome. Just a day and a half left and I'd made the error of staying the wrong side of the river, in Marconi, thinking it would be easy enough to get to the Via Appia not far away across the Tiber. Big mistake. Where I'd landed up was fine as a hotel and a local area but modern Rome in a nutshell. The streets were full of litter, the traffic so choked I waited for a bus for nearly half an hour and still it didn't come.

The amiable receptionist at the hotel lived out in Ariccia and drove to work daily, an hour each way. She couldn't afford to live in the city and didn't like the bustle anyway. The traffic, it seemed, was awful throughout the day and needed police officers standing in the road to ease the jams. In the end, the only way I could get out was to make a long walk to Trastevere station and hop on a tram there. Rome had become a tangle of choked streets and buses that never showed. Two lessons learned. First, pick where you stay according to where you want to go. Second... there's never any rushing this place. It's not just that the city of two thousand years ago was so large and, today, so difficult in parts to travel. Rome possesses a multitude of layers, fascinating dark corners that only reveal themselves just when you think you're done. There's a saying... *non basta una vita*. One lifetime isn't enough. If the locals feel that way, what hope is there for the rest of us?

I'd spent countless months there over the years researching novels and studying at a language college. But now I understood I'd barely scratched the surface. I'd run out of time, which was why, a few months later after setting down my notes and thoughts, I found myself back on Appius's road, this time on a cold January day, trying to see it more clearly.

WHEN APPIUS'S heirs reached that point by the harbour in Brindisi marked by those columns by the house where Virgil died, Rome was lifting its head and starting to take an avaricious look beyond its own borders, at the world outside. That relentless hunger would define it for the next five hundred years. The last mile of the Via Appia by the Adriatic was in many ways the beginning of this story. Just as the start of the road, that dead-straight line running out from the Porta Capena, through the Porta San Sebastiano in the Aurelian Walls and out into the countryside, would come to provide its end.

For many this stretch is all they know of the Via Appia, a well-preserved and popular public monument that represents just a fraction of the original. A trip to the area has been an essential tick on visitors' itineraries for centuries. Back in the days of the Grand Tour, when the gentry of England set off to do all the great sights of Europe in one go, lords and ladies, the rich and the artistic, all flocked here to touch the hem of Imperial Rome.

Not everyone enjoyed it. Charles Dickens found his visit a touch depressing.

> *Tombs and temples, overthrown and prostrate; small fragments of columns, friezes, pediments; great blocks of granite and marble; mouldering arches, grass-grown and decayed; ruin enough to build a spacious city from; lay strewn about us... The aspect of the desolate Campagna in one direction, where it was most level, reminded me of an American prairie; but what is the solitude of a region where men have never dwelt, to that of a Desert, where a mighty race have left their footprints in the earth from which they have vanished; where the resting-places of their Dead, have fallen like their Dead; and the broken hour-glass of Time is but a heap of idle dust!*

That's a bit histrionic for me. It must have been a very high, hot summer if he felt the fields around the road looked like prairies. Still, Dickens did touch upon something very real: the dead do lurk around these parts, in two very different forms: the obvious and the hidden.

Given how freely they killed people, the Romans were decidedly funny about death. They were constantly bothered by what they saw as bad omens. This greatly annoyed Cicero, a rationalist, at least in his own head. He wrote an entire book rubbishing the idea of divination, concluding, 'If we're going to accept chance utterances of this kind as omens, we had better look out when we stumble, or break a shoelace, or sneeze!'

He was in the minority. Emperors were as hooked on superstition as the man or woman in the street, forever looking for clues about the future in the prophecies of astrologers and haruspicy, the practice of fortune-telling from the liver of a newly slaughtered animal. The risk of death was to be avoided at all costs, but when Romans, high or low, passed to the next world, they very much wanted people to remember them. The lavish spectacle and ceremony around funerals was lampooned by the writer Petronius in his late first century bawdy story

Satyricon. Trimalchio, a pompous, *nouveau riche* figure of ridicule, is drunk and issuing orders for his funeral.

> *I am appointing one of the freedmen to be caretaker of the tomb and prevent the common people from running up and crapping on it. I beg you to put ships in full sail on the monument, and me sitting in official robes on my official seat, wearing five gold rings and distributing coin publicly out of a bag... I should like a dining-room table put in too, if you can arrange it. And let me have the whole people there enjoying themselves. On my right hand put a statue of dear Fortunata holding a dove, and let her be leading a little dog with a waistband on; and my dear little boy, and big jars sealed with gypsum, so that the wine may not run out. And have a broken urn carved with a boy weeping over it. And a sundial in the middle, so that anyone who looks at the time will read my name whether he likes it or not... 'Here lies Caius Pompeius Trimalchio, freedman of Maecenas.'*

It's all a joke. He's dead drunk, not dead. But this tale typifies the importance Romans who'd found a little prosperity – former slaves among them – placed on leaving a memory of themselves behind. And where better than the Via Appia, the Queen of Roads, the most important highway in the empire? The teeming hordes who crowded it travelling north and south deserved to be impressed. When they finally arrived in the city they'd be greeted by the vast magnificence of the Circus Maximus, the palaces on the Palatine, the grand and pointless folly of the Septizodium, and the Colosseum round the corner.

How could anyone with the cash pass up the opportunity to take away the breath of passing visitors with a monumental tomb of their own?

❦ 18 ❦

THE ROAD OF THE DEAD

THE HISTORIC AREA surrounding the Via Appia as it leaves Rome falls under the care of the Parco Regionale dell'Appia Antica, some 3400 hectares of open countryside, the odd built-up area, and walks so rural it's hard to believe a crowded metropolis is a few miles away. There's so much to see here, some of it well-known and occasionally over-crowded, other parts barely visited. You could easily spend days and a lot of shoe leather exploring its many aspects then go home rueing what you'd missed.

Churches, imperial villas, tombs, play parks for children, aqueducts, trails and cycle paths, some of the most beautiful Roman frescoes around... they're all there, well-served by buses from the centre of Rome, and with several places to hire bikes, pedal or electric, one of the best ways to get around where there aren't too many cars about.

But first let's take a slight detour from the Via Appia, along the road that preceded it, the Via Latina which goes back to prehistory, running all the way from what was once a little Rome, 120 miles to Capua. Too slow, too winding in parts for the likes of Appius Claudius Caecus, desperate to speed his troops and supplies to the front in Campania.

The Latina is still there close to the city, an elderly relative to the

Appia following the same route before splitting north after the Baths of Caracalla. It's the narrow street that runs beside the park on the other side of the Scipio tombs, the place to find that curious little octagonal church where John the Evangelist supposedly survived being boiled in oil by Domitian. The emperor, the last of the Flavians and a particularly nasty example of his kind, later returned to the area as a blood-stained corpse after he was stabbed to death in an ugly court conspiracy that ended in a knife fight with his attackers. His body was taken by his old wet nurse Phyllis and cremated in the garden of her suburban villa on the Via Latina not far from the spot where he tried to cook a saint.

Afterwards Phyllis mixed his ashes with those of his mistress Julia, daughter to the emperor Titus who she'd raised too, and interred them together in a temple near his former home on the Quirinal hill. But the hated Domitian was subjected to *damnatio memoriae* which meant every trace of him, memorials, coins, statues, was to be erased from sight. The tomb was probably one of the first to go.

You can see what *damnatio memoriae* means through two impressive bas-reliefs in the Vatican Museums known as the Cancelleria Reliefs. These were originally commissioned by Domitian to depict his glorious life and the famed history of the Flavian dynasty founded by his father Vespasian. But if you look at some of the faces meant to represent him, it's clear someone has taken a chisel to them and tried to change his appearance to that of his successor, Nerva. This nabbing of credit from a deceased predecessor is a habit we're going to meet again very soon.

The road passes through the old gate of the Porta Latina in the Aurelian Walls. It then becomes an ordinary suburban street until we reach the Caffarella park which forms a largely green triangle of Roman history with the Via Appia to the south. It's worth reading up on the itineraries on the regional park website. This vast area can be tackled in many different ways, on foot along a network of paths, by bus, by bike, even by hired golf caddy. Walking or cycling is best but you need to plan. The distances can be confusing. From the Porta Latina of the old road to the Porta San Sebastiano of the Appia, for example, is only a six or seven-minute stroll. From the Porta San Sebastiano to one of the major sights of the Appia, the tomb of Caecilia Metella, is a couple of miles and a good half hour – thankfully there are buses to take you there.

The easiest route to Caffarella is to hop on the 87 from the city centre and get off at the stop marked De Sanctis. This is nothing like as historic as it sounds, but you're one block from the Latina and the park which runs all the way down to the Appia. It's not the best-labelled place around – the reception centre is basically a friendly bike hire shop where you can pick up a few pamphlets. But Google Maps will guide you along the footpaths to the sights. Caffarella is an oasis for joggers and dog walkers, families enjoying the picnic and barbecue areas, most of whom blithely go past its history without a second thought. A squawking throng of bright green feral parakeets sometimes sweeps through the trees to add a lurid, exotic flavour to the atmosphere. There's also the Casale della Vaccareccia, a historic farm that grazes a large flock of sheep on the verdant meadows fed by the Almone river. You can buy fresh home-made pecorino and ricotta from the flock if you find the shop is open.

The Romans of old adored this area. It was peaceful, scattered with sacred sites, perfect for a country bolthole. In its heyday this was home to estates belonging to the emperors and the very rich, all keen to get out of the bustle and squalor of the city. Archaeological remains are scattered round the park like toys thrown out of an ancient god's pram. A nymphaeum? Track down the one supposedly dedicated to the nymph of the Almone river, Egeria, a picturesque watery complex, probably from the second century AD, hidden away in the woods. In reality, this was probably a garden feature on the estate of a rich and powerful second century politician called Herodes Atticus who owned most of the land around this part of the Via Appia. Not far away the waters of the Almone provide the spring for the local mineral water named after the nymph, all bottled in a busy plant open to the public at the edge of the park.

Hidden away in the depths of Caffarella stands the church of Sant'Urbano, very much in the style of an ancient Roman temple, as it should be since it occupies the site of just such a building erected by Herodes Atticus in memory of his late wife. Today's church is mostly a seventeenth century restoration, but inside there's a second century pagan altar with a snake circling round the shaft. Though you'll probably have to take my word on that since the place is usually closed and the best you can do is peer through the fence.

The most spectacular Roman remains in the area lie a little way away, on the other side of the busy modern Via Appia Nuova. There you'll find a short stretch of the original Via Latina with some second century tombs complete with stucco work and frescoes. It's a lovely spot, secluded beneath stone pines, and probably a sight closer to the feel of the original outlying reaches of the Via Appia near the city than the modern tourist-oriented road itself. The park is open most days, but to see inside the tombs you need to book for one of the openings – currently only at weekends.

Wander a little further, on the other side of the highway, and you'll soon find yourself being led astray into the area known as the Seven Aqueducts. This is a setting beloved of film makers, full of the remains of the astonishing structures built to bring water into the city. Perhaps the most spectacular, the Claudio, begun by Caligula and finished by his uncle Claudius, ran for around forty five miles from modern Subiaco into the imperial palaces of the Palatine itself.

Then, close by the fifth milestone of the Via Appia, there are the ruins of the Villa of the Quintilii, home to two wealthy aristocratic brothers who built themselves an estate so grand and well-placed that the emperor Commodus took a shine to it, had the pair murdered, and seized the property for himself. It's quite a pile, with a museum, a nymphaeum and lovely views. Most of the valuable archaeological finds are, however, to be found in the British Museum.

If you've wandered this far, then you are in danger of falling victim to the perennial problem that faces all Rome lovers: every time you go back the place seems to get bigger. So plan your day, enjoy these peripheral pleasures, then focus on the main task in hand. The chances are you're going to run out of time for that too.

ENOUGH OF THE EARLIER HIGHWAY. Now back to the main event: the Via Appia Antica.

The first thing to say is that much of what's on show in this stretch near Rome is fake, a recreation, ruins exhumed from the ground, primped and primed for public consumption. The Appia began to fall into disuse in the fifth century as the Roman Empire started to collapse. In its prime, the road was maintained by a highly-organised bureaucracy and a system of taxation that funded its repair. When that vanished, so did the engineers and workers needed to keep it going. Marshland encroached, cobbles were never replaced. Centuries later towns along the length of the road were ravaged by Saracen attacks. The last portion to survive was this stretch leading into the capital. But when the popes began to build great churches in the city and move holy relics from their original resting places on the Via Appia into their basilicas, the pilgrims vanished too.

A more worldly form of tourism was, in part, the Via Appia's saviour. More than a millennium on, all the wealthy foreigners coming to experience the grandeur of Rome were very vocal when it came to complaining about the neglect of the city's monuments. With support from the Pontifical Government, Roman architects and artists, among them the sculptor Canova, set about reviving the 'Queen of Roads'.

The first ten miles we see today are largely the creation of Luigi Canina, the Commissioner of Antiquities for the city in the middle of the nineteenth century. Canina excavated tombs and villas and built the low walls which still run alongside the road – the original had nothing like them. He also took an imaginative approach to dealing with what he found. By the side of today's road you'll come across fragments of tombs and monuments mounted in brick surrounds, pieces of an unknown past placed there for show. Again, none of this reflects what the road was like before.

The pagans – everyone who wasn't Christian – wanted their graves above ground, visible proof of their lives for all passing travellers to see. In its pomp, the Via Appia would have been a procession of temple-like tombs stretching for miles on both sides. We've already met one of the most important, the mausoleum of the Scipios. At first glance this seems to break the Roman rule set out in the ancient Law of the Twelve Tables which dictated that the dead had to be interred outside the city walls. In fact, the site of the monument simply demonstrates the way Rome expanded. The Scipios put down their marker not long after the first stretch of the Via Appia was built in 312 BC. At that point, their necropolis was outside the city walls.

A good first stop on any initial exploration of the Appia is the point at which it emerges through the Aurelian wall, the Porta San Sebastiano. Hop off the bus close by and you have access to the twin towers that have stood over this part of the city periphery for around 1800 years in one form or another. Inside there's a small museum about the walls, and the chance to stroll the parapets for fine views back to the city and ahead to the Alban Hills.

The tombs of the mighty, the wealthy and some very ordinary folk crowded the highway for miles. The circular monument of Crassus's daughter-in-law, Caecilia Metella, is one of the remaining highlights, a vast white drum, with the ruins of a medieval castle next to it. On foot you notice this appears to be on one of the rare hills along this stretch of the Appia. In fact, it's not a normal hill at all – the tomb sits on one of the lava outflows from an ancient volcanic eruption around Albano. Originally the structure would have had a conical roof rising to twenty metres. But that's gone and in its place are military crenellations added when the building was turned into a fortified village. This was a medieval development, one which passed through the hands of some of Rome's most famous families, among them the Colonna, the Orsini and the Caetani. Hard as it is to imagine today, it once represented a formidable barrier across this stretch of the Via Appia, a military stronghold that stopped every traveller moving to and from the city. Holding the fort of Caecilia Metella was usually a privilege of whatever clan controlled the territory south – and took the dues of anyone using the road.

Plenty of famous names have monuments attributed to them nearby. Atticus, the constant correspondent of Cicero, was buried in a family tomb at the fifth mile. A lump of brickwork near the nineteenth century Forte Appia is supposedly all that remains of the tomb of Seneca the Younger who opened his veins in a bath after being ordered to commit suicide by his former pupil, Nero. The memorial often called the tomb of Pompey is a burial site for the former general's family, not the man himself. According to Plutarch, his ashes were given to his wife after he was beheaded in Egypt while fleeing Julius Caesar. She buried them in the villa they had in the Alban Hills, now part of the Pope's summer palace at Castel Gandolfo.

One emperor was certainly buried close by. At the ninth mile, where there was a *mutatio*, a stop for a change of horses, stand the ruins of a circular mausoleum for Gallienus who had the misfortune to rule for fifteen years, the first seven with his father Valerian, during the time the wheels started to come off the empire in the late third century. Gallienus was stabbed to death by one of his commanders outside Milan during a siege. A marginally preferable end to that of his father who was captured by the Persians and used as a living footstool before being either forced to swallow molten gold or flayed. After which his skin was stuffed with straw and his corpse used as a temple decoration.

But it wasn't just the posh and the rich who wanted to leave their mark. Look carefully around the city and you'll find monuments left by ordinary people, ones who'd made a bit of money and wanted the world to know. One of my favourites is built into the remains of the Aurelian Wall at Porta Maggiore. It belonged to a chap called Eurysaces, probably a former slave who later became a popular and successful baker. A frieze depicts the baking process, from sifting flour to kneading dough, then placing loaves in what looks very much like the domed pizza oven used today.

There's nothing quite so fancy from an ordinary Roman on the Via Appia. But at the fifth mile you'll find a marble tablet left by another former slave, a dealer in pearls who once worked on the Via Sacra in the centre of the Forum, 'Stop traveller and look at this mound on the left where the bones of a good man are enclosed, one compassionate, devoted and fond of the poor. I ask you traveller, do not harm this tomb.'

There are even monuments to loyal dogs, with soppy epigraphs for lost pets. The inscription on one reads, 'Guardian of the wagons, he never barked without reason, now he is silent and a shadow watches over his ashes.'

Also at the fifth mile you'll find a poem that's a direct message from the man whose ashes once resided within the ruined tomb there.

This memorial was made for Marcus Caecilius.
Thank you, dear guest, for stopping at my home.
Good luck and good health to you. Sleep without a care.

It's not exactly the message Spike Milligan left on his headstone... *I told you I was ill.* But there is a stoic, rational, almost light-hearted approach to death in many Roman funeral epitaphs. Cicero, discussing the problems of old age, declared, 'I depart from life, as from an inn, not as from a home; for nature has given us here a lodging for a sojourn, not a place of habitation.' When his time came outside his villa in Formia, he acknowledged it and held out his neck for the executioner.

Sleep without a care.

Death doesn't just lurk above the ground in those few miles of the Via Appia as it leaves the city. It's hidden away beneath the green fields and the monuments too. In a faith traditional Rome, with its many gods, imported from all over the empire, would first treat with suspicion, repression and persecution, then embrace above all others.

19

ONE GOD AND ONE ALONE

And from thence, when the brethren heard of us, they came to meet us as far as Appii Forum, and The Three Taverns: whom when Paul saw, he thanked God, and took courage. Acts 28 15.

IT'S JUST a pile of stones by a pretty stretch of the Via Appia now. But two thousand years ago Tres Tabernae – 'Three Taverns' – was a busy stop along the road. Forum Appii we've met already – it was the place where Horace encountered those drunken, cheating boatmen. He and his mates had taken two days to get there through laziness, he noted. Most people did it in one. Tres Tabernae was closer to Rome, near the modern town of Cisterna di Latina. Countless Christians must have travelled along the Via Appia over the centuries, but these are the only two places the bible mentions by name.

Augustus lived for a while in Tres Tabernae. An emperor few people have ever heard of, Valerius Severus, was either executed or forced to commit suicide there in 307 AD after a miserable year in the job. His nemesis, Maxentius, would shortly meet his own violent fate. The world was a touch more settled when Paul of Tarsus, the future saint, turned up to be met by his fellow Christians around two hundred and fifty years earlier. There are stories aplenty about Roman persecution of Christians, but what's less commonly understood is that they were getting a hard time back in Jerusalem too. Paul had only just escaped with his life there after being attacked by a Jewish sect, then saved by a bunch of Roman centurions who intervened and dragged him in front of a local judge.

Faced with prosecution, he opted for trial in Rome, as was his right as a citizen. He then embarked upon a difficult journey, which included being shipwrecked in Malta, before turning up in Italy at Puteoli in the Bay of Naples. From there he travelled up the Via Appia to be met by his followers in Tres Tabernae, then on to Rome.

At the time, Christians were mostly tolerated as one more slightly weird foreign cult. The city had lots of different religions to choose from. Most citizens seemed to think they should be allowed to pick the one they wanted. Those in power didn't mind so long as no one upset the status quo. Paul's offence was that he'd acquired the reputation of being a troublemaker, someone who inflamed emotions and questioned authority. These were not practices the Roman state ever liked.

Then, in 64 AD, came the Great Fire of Rome, a six-day inferno that tore through the teeming, overcrowded metropolis, ripping through the tinder of its wooden buildings, leaving mangled ruins in its wake. As much as two thirds of the city was destroyed. It was only natural that people would want someone to blame.

The historian Tacitus was eight years old when the blaze happened and is adamant that Nero made a conscious decision to use the Christians as scapegoats. Suetonius, born five years later, came to the same conclusion. One reason Nero might have tried to blame others was that rumours had spread that he'd started the fire himself and sang (not played the violin which didn't then exist) while it happened. That he'd wanted old Rome destroyed so he could build a new version of it in the Greek style he preferred. Nero followed his great uncle Claudius onto the imperial throne, supposedly after his mum Agrippina, who'd married the old man in a decidedly dodgy union, poisoned her husband's beloved mushrooms at a banquet. On the throne he made Caligula seem like a well-balanced chap with just a few personal eccentricities. If you believe all the stories, by the time of the fire he'd already murdered his mother and stepbrother, Claudius's son, executed countless upper class Romans and his ex-wife, and outraged Roman society by dressing as a bride and marrying a male slave in public. He was out of the city having a seaside break in Antium (Anzio) at the time of the fire. But he didn't quell the rumours much when he used the devastation caused by the blaze to build himself a vast new palace, the Domus Aurea or Golden House, on the ruins.

The scale of this was astonishing. Imagine an enormous Roman Versailles, a complex of extraordinary palaces and exotic gardens occupying much of the ground that was once home to the cramped wooden terraces that vanished in the fire. You can get some insight into its size and excess by booking a visit to the excavations in the park opposite the Colosseum – and this is only a fraction of the original. When it was rediscovered at the end of the fifteenth century buried beneath the Esquiline Hill, artists like Michelangelo and Raphael scrambled down ropes to enter the grottoes beneath and study the elaborate frescoes that adorned the walls. The term 'grotesque' in art originated in the Domus Aurea, from the Italian *grottesche* meaning from a cave.

Nero's Golden House extended across much of this part of Rome, from the Esquiline Hill to the Palatine. In the valley he created an artificial lake with pavilions and boats on the site of what later became the Colosseum. It's not hard to imagine what the average working Roman, living in relative squalor and poverty, must have made of the place. The demented emperor's reckless profligacy didn't go down well with locals still struggling to find their feet after most of their city had been razed to charred timbers and ashes. So, to kill the rumour that he'd started the fire, he turned on the Christians.

Tacitus takes up the tale...

Nero fastened the guilt and inflicted the most exquisite tortures on a class hated for their abominations, called Christians by the populace. Christus, from whom the name had its origin, suffered the extreme penalty during the reign of Tiberius at the hands of one of our procurators, Pontius Pilatus, and a most mischievous superstition, thus checked for the moment, again broke out not only in Judea, the first source of the evil, but even in Rome, where all things hideous and shameful from every part of the world find their centre and become popular.

Accordingly, an arrest was first made of all who pleaded guilty; then, upon their information, an immense multitude was convicted, not so much of the crime of firing the city, as of hatred against mankind.

What followed was public agony and execution.

Mockery of every sort was added to their deaths. Covered with the skins of beasts, they were torn apart by dogs and perished, or were nailed to crosses, or were doomed to the flames and burnt, to serve as a nightly illumination, when daylight had expired. Nero offered his gardens for the spectacle, and was exhibiting a show in the circus, while he mingled with the people in the dress of a charioteer or stood aloft on a car. Hence, even for criminals who deserved extreme and exemplary punishment, there arose a feeling of compassion; for it was not, as it seemed, for the public good, but to glut one man's cruelty, that they were being destroyed.

Paul was among the victims, beheaded and buried close to his execution. A tomb that bears his name can be found in the church of San Paolo fuori le Mura on the Via Ostiense.

His fellow apostle Peter is commemorated in the most famous basilica in the world, the heart of the Vatican, built on the spot where he was said to have been crucified upside down because he felt himself unworthy of dying in the same way as Christ. The Egyptian column in the piazza of Saint Peter's supposedly witnessed his death when it was part of the stadium Nero had built in the area.

In fact, the New Testament never places Peter in Rome. Whether he went there or not, he left his mark. Close to the Porta San Sebastiano, on a scruffy stretch of the Appia that's often choked with traffic, there's a bus stop next to a bike hire shop and a local restaurant. On the other side of the road is a small white church known as Domine Quo Vadis. There's nothing particularly notable about it except a marble slab which bears the imprint of two bare feet. Archaeologists will tell you these are a piece of Roman statuary, and you'll find examples much like it in the Capitoline museum. The church has another story. Peter, afraid for his life, decided to flee the city along the Via Appia and make his way back to the Holy Land. As he reached the spot where the church now stands an apparition of Christ appeared before him. A shocked Peter asked, '*Domine, quo vadis?*' Lord, where are you going? The apparition replied, '*Eo Romam iterum crucifigi.*' I am going to Rome to be crucified again. Duly admonished for his cowardice, Peter turned back and returned to the city and his martyrdom. The holy footsteps Jesus made remained as proof of his spectral visit.

Pilgrims occasionally kiss the marble footprints in Domine Quo Vadis, unaware they're actually a copy; the original is in the church of San Sebastiano up the road. Close by is a small circular building that commemorates a later form of cruelty. The 'Cappella di Reginald Pole' is named after an English Catholic priest who fled his home after falling foul of Henry VIII when the king wanted a divorce and was set on leaving the church of Rome and establishing one of his own. Henry hated Pole and sent a team of assassins to murder him in Italy. The attempt failed and this little chapel was Pole's way of saying thanks to god for saving him from the English king's killers.

Henry didn't give up. When he couldn't get his hands on Reginald he went for his mother, Margaret, the Countess of Salisbury, who was convicted on a trumped-up charge of treason and messily beheaded in the Tower of London at the age of sixty seven, proclaiming her innocence all along. Tyranny and cruelty were not for Roman emperors alone. Still, Pole had the last laugh in a way. After Henry died his daughter Mary turned England back to Rome, removed the attainder against Pole, brought him home and made him Archbishop of Canterbury, the last Catholic to hold the post. The priest who built that little circular temple to celebrate his escape from an English king's killers is now buried in the Corona of Canterbury Cathedral, the shrine built to house the remains of Saint Thomas Becket until a vengeful Henry VIII had his 350-year-old bones removed on charges of treason.

There's a lot of faith and plenty of death hereabouts. Far more than meets the eye on the symmetrical old cobbles above the ground. Building roads, as we now know, has unexpected consequences. All around this stretch of the Via Appia there were once quarries to produce the stone for the road itself. The followers of Peter and Paul, who would come to number more than fifty thousand in Rome in the space of little more than a century, didn't want their dead cremated, their ashes kept in urns above ground. They demanded their loved ones be buried beneath the earth.

Those empty workings by the road provided an obvious opportunity to create what they called a *coemeterium*, 'a place of rest'. A cemetery, as the word has come down to us. Another term based on Latin would find its way into the dictionary for the tunnels they would create through those workings on the Via Appia and come to be applied to underground burial sites around the world: *catacumbae*.

Catacombs.

THE 118 BUS drops you off close to the two best-known sets of catacombs on the Via Appia, those of San Callisto and San Sebastiano, just half a mile apart. From the road, there's nothing to indicate the scale of the network of tombs beneath your feet. San Callisto's extend to ninety acres and a network of galleries twelve miles long beneath the ground. In the third century it was the official burial place for the Church of Rome. At least nine early popes and a number of martyrs were buried there, along with perhaps as many as half a million – yes, *half a million* – others.

A busy coach park sits next to the modern building coping with pilgrims and the curious. After you buy your ticket you're asked to wait in queues according to language. Twenty minutes later a charming Filipino guide – a Vatican priest in civilian clothing it turned out – took us down a series of steps into the web of tunnels below.

A visit to catacombs is always going to be organised. It's dark down there in parts, even with lighting. The tunnels are so narrow that those with a fear of confined spaces can get spooked. Then, from time to time, you come across the very obvious evidence of human remains. 'I will shortly show you some bones,' the guide announced more than once as we approached some sad pieces of bleached skeleton lurking in the corners of the tombs.

To be honest, the tours here, and the nearby San Sebastiano catacombs, take place at such a pace it's hard to keep up with the complexity of what you're seeing. Both have a lot of tourists to process, so you're underground for forty five minutes at best. You're rushing past a lot of history in that time. In Callisto there's the tomb of the early popes, five of them, including Sixtus II executed by Valerian, the emperor who ended up stuffed with straw in a temple in Persia.

One of the most surprising discoveries is the cavity that was once the grave of Saint Cecilia, a young woman martyred in the third century. Five hundred years later her relics were exhumed to be transferred to the church in Trastevere where they remain. Cue one of those spooky stories the church loves so much. The men who came to move her body found the saint 'incorrupt', untouched by age, wrapped in a silk shroud, face down, hands out in front of her, the axe cuts that took her life clearly visible.

In 1599, preparing for the Holy Year to come, Pope Clement VIII ordered her tomb to be reopened. She was still in the same unspoilt state and the men responsible for the work reported a 'mysterious and delightful flower-like odour which proceeded from the coffin'. The pope commissioned one of the most famous sculptors of the day, Stefano Maderno, to make an exact copy of her figure. The original is still in the church named after her in Trastevere, but a very good copy lies in the space where she was originally found in the Callisto tunnels. Maderno said of his work, 'Behold the body of the most holy virgin Cecilia whom I myself saw lying incorrupt in her tomb. I have in this marble expressed for you the same saint in the very same posture of body.'

Even for a diehard atheist like me it's a moving sight, the young woman's figure so real, so seemingly recent, she might have died yesterday. I was in the midst of a bunch of happy tourists when we were led into that small chamber where her prone statue occupies a niche on the floor. Everyone fell silent in an instant. Cecilia's church in Trastevere is supposedly built over the Roman house in which she lived, singing as she was tortured, which is why she's now the patron saint of music. It's a beautiful, quiet place, somewhere the tourist masses rarely find, and still with a strong musical connection.

The San Sebastiano catacombs have a different atmosphere, more organised and formal since they sit beneath a large and ancient church that was rendered rather unremarkable during a seventeenth century reconstruction. Nor will you encounter a trace of bones, at least as far as I've seen. Above ground in the basilica sits the last sculpture by Bernini, a head of Christ executed when the artist was eighty years old. It's technically brilliant, naturally, but makes Jesus look like an elegant cavalier with a well-kept beard and flowing locks. The 'real' footsteps of Christ originally in the Quo Vadis church down the road are here too, along with the altar containing the remains of Sebastian.

He was a Gaul who became an army captain under Diocletian. When it was discovered he was a Christian converting other soldiers he was shot by the emperor's archers, an image that inspired countless artists during the Renaissance and spurred a busy pilgrim trade to the Via Appia. Sebastian pierced with arrows is generally seen to be his martyrdom. But it's not as simple as that. Legend has it he miraculously survived his wounds and was nursed back to health by a pious woman who took pity on him, Saint Irene. Recovered and still determined to prove his faith, Sebastian then sought out Diocletian and gave him an earful in public over his mistreatment of the Christians. After which, to no one's great surprise, he was beaten to death and thrown into the Cloaca Maxima, the principal sewer of Rome. His spirit appeared in a dream to another Christian woman who recovered his corpse and buried him in the catacombs on the Via Appia as he'd requested.

San Sebastiano is much more interesting below the ground than above. The tour takes in a winding itinerary past tombs and niches until you reach the small chapel where the body of Sebastian was originally kept. The remains of Peter and Paul were interred here too, or so the stories have it, worshipped in secret when the Roman authorities were stamping on all public shows of faith. For me, the real highlights, however, are three second-century family mausolea, roofed like small temples or houses. They once sat outside in a depression of the quarry which preceded the church. Then, as the complex grew, they were covered in earth for centuries, which is why they remain relatively well-preserved. Delicate frescoes run around the walls and the niches for the deceased. These little homes for the dead have a touching sense of family about them you won't find elsewhere.

So... Callisto or Sebastiano? It's hard to choose. The visits last less than an hour. They're each fascinating, and quite different in atmosphere. For me, Callisto has the edge. It's more mysterious and that statue of Cecilia is simply stunning. Sebastiano has a more formal appeal, but those three mausolea are quite something too. So if you have the time... both, perhaps on different days.

THE CATACOMBS WEREN'T JUST burial places. There were areas for church services and family gatherings to mark the annual day of the dead. The common belief that whole communities of Christians hid there to escape the persecutions above ground is one more Roman myth. For one thing, the atmosphere is quite unhealthy due to the constant seeping of sulphuric volcanic fumes into the chambers. Our guide was keen to point that out when we were down below. Catacomb staff like him were told they could only stay underground safely for a few hours a day.

In any case, because the persecution was sporadic, not constant, there would be little need to hide from sight most of the time. Some historians believe that, over the three centuries from the crucifixion to the broad legalisation of Christianity, the number of people executed for their faith ran to a few thousand at most. Compared to the mass slaughters the Romans committed elsewhere – in Jerusalem, in Britain, in Gaul and Germany – this is a tiny number. Besides, trapped below ground in a warren of tunnels a few miles outside the city walls, they would hardly be difficult to find for any army troop that wished to attack them.

Why did the Romans pick on the Christians in the first place? Even though this happened two thousand years ago we can get a very direct insight into their thinking through some high level official correspondence. An astonishing amount still exists, including an exchange between one senior official and his boss in Rome. It dates back to 112

AD when Pliny the Younger was governor of a province in Anatolia, sent there by the emperor Trajan.

Pliny was a fellow with a habit for being close to events. As an eighteen-year-old in 79 AD he'd witnessed the eruption of Vesuvius from across the Bay of Naples and left us a first-hand account of what it looked like from afar. His more famous uncle, Pliny the Elder, wrote one of the first books on science and nature and was the commander of the Roman fleet in the area at the time of the eruption. He died trying to help people trapped in the disaster.

Thirty three years later, now a senior official of the state, Pliny decided he needed some advice about how to deal with the pesky cultists who followed a convicted and executed criminal from Bethlehem. So he asked the man at the top, the emperor, Trajan.

It is my custom, Sir, to refer to you in all cases where I do not feel sure, for who can better direct my doubts or inform my ignorance... In the meantime, this is the plan which I have adopted in the case of those Christians who have been brought before me. I ask them whether they are Christians; if they say yes, then I repeat the question a second and a third time, warning them of the penalties it entails, and if they still persist, I order them to be taken away for execution. For I do not doubt that, whatever the character of the crime may be which they confess, their pertinacity and inflexible obstinacy certainly ought to be punished... Those who denied that they were or had been Christians and called upon the gods in the usual formula, reciting the words after me, those who offered incense and wine before your image, which I had given orders to be brought forward for this purpose, together with the statues of the deities – all such I considered should be discharged, especially as they cursed the name of Christ, which, it is said, those who are really Christians cannot be induced to do...

I thought it the more necessary, therefore, to find out what truth there was in these statements by submitting two women, who were called deaconesses, to the torture, but I found nothing but a debased superstition carried to great lengths... the contagion of this superstition has spread not only through the free cities, but into the villages and the rural districts, and yet it seems to me that it can be checked and set right.

In short, a puzzled Pliny had Christians brought before him and asked them three times to give up their faith. If they refused to pray to the Roman gods, to offer up wine in front of the emperor's image and insult the name of Christ, they were executed. Or, in the case of Roman citizens, sent to Rome for judgement if they so wished – which was what happened to Paul of Tarsus. Pliny declares the Christians' 'pertinacity and inflexible obstinacy certainly ought to be punished'. Even, it seems, if there's no real evidence of any actual crime except being Christian.

Trajan had banned anything he saw as a political 'fraternity' on the basis that it might prove the breeding ground of subversion. Christianity fitted the description because its followers met in private, kept their own company and followed practices that were outside normal Roman behaviour. Perhaps the last is the real 'crime'. Christians were different. They followed one god, a strict moral regime, and refused to conform to the mores of the empire. Romans were, without a doubt, great control freaks. They may have taken a liberal attitude in private to sexual matters and everyday corruption. But, when it came to politics and matters of state, conformity was everything – and the Christians simply refused to play ball.

Trajan's reply is revealing.

You have adopted the proper course, my dear Pliny, in examining the cases of those who have been denounced to you as Christians, for no hard and fast rule can be laid down to meet a question of such wide extent. The Christians are not to be hunted out; if they are brought before you and the offence is proved, they are to be punished, but with this reservation – that if anyone denies that he is a Christian and makes it clear that he is not, by offering prayers to our deities, then he is to be pardoned because of his recantation, however suspicious his past conduct may have been. But accusations published anonymously must not carry any weight whatever, no matter what the charge may be, for they are not only a precedent of the very worst type, but they are not in consonance with the spirit of our age.

He sounds a lot less concerned about the matter than his anxious servant in distant Anatolia. Don't seek Christians out, don't listen to anonymous tittle-tattle, pardon anyone if they swear to the old gods, execute them if they're stubborn.

It didn't work. As the years went by the ranks of Christians in Rome swelled. It's a myth to think they were constantly at risk of persecution, forever being dragged off to the arena to face gladiators or wild beasts. There may have been local discrimination against minorities in parts of the empire – and not just Christians but Jews as well. But an organised, central campaign of persecution happened only sporadically. Nero was the first, looking for scapegoats for the disastrous fire in order to divert suspicion from himself. Yet half a century later the emperor Hadrian was issuing orders that Christians were not to be persecuted unless they broke the law, and anyone who tried to get them indicted should be tried instead.

How much persecution came from the top, rather than simple local prejudice, is hard to establish. Septimius Severus, one of those rare emperors who died of natural causes, in York after visiting Hadrian's Wall, is cited as a persecutor of Christians by one church historian Eusebius and as someone who intervened personally to save Christians from execution by another, Tertullian. It may be that Tertullian, a son of Carthage, felt warmly towards Severus who was a fellow north African. But Tertullian was also a great fan of martyrdom in the furtherance of Christianity. One of his sayings that has come down to us is, 'The blood of the martyrs is the seed of the church.' So if he thought Severus was a good guy... perhaps he was.

Valerian certainly took against the Christians, executing bishops and ordinary worshippers alike before he was captured by the Persians and wound up stuffed with straw in a temple. In 303 Diocletian initiated the harshest period of persecution, issuing an edict that ordered the destruction of churches and Christian literature and banning all meetings. He emphasised this should be done without violence, but quite a few local governors weren't listening. The empire itself was starting to crumble, with different contenders appearing in the hope of seizing power. Some were in favour of tolerance. Others of stamping out all but the traditional cults. Whether Christians lived or died depended on where and when they happened to find themselves.

And all the while Tertullian's words proved true. The blood of the martyrs really was the seed of the church. The more men and women stood up for their faith and suffered oppression and the ultimate penalty as a result, the more recruits flocked to the new monotheistic religion from the east. There are no hard and fast figures for the Christian population of Rome around this time. No one kept the numbers. But there seems good reason to believe that they represented a few per cent of the city's population in the year 250, and the majority a century later. Perhaps the recurring crises in the state tempted people to give up on the old gods and try their faith with a new one, a solitary deity who promised salvation, peace and harmony.

A Roman who lived in the greatest luxury not far from the catacombs of Callisto and San Sebastiano would soon help turn that steady trickle into a flood which would one day cover much of the world.

20

ROME'S LAST DAYS

By the beginning of the fourth century, the Roman Empire was split into four parts. Italy, Spain and North Africa were under the control of a senior emperor dubbed Augustus. A second Augustus controlled the east, from Egypt through Byzantium to the Black Sea. A junior figure known as 'Caesar' ran Britain and Gaul while his counterpart had control of Greece and the Balkans. This was known as a 'tetrarchy', from the Greek meaning government by four.

If you want a rough idea of what they looked like you need to take yourself off to Venice, stand in the Piazza San Marco and locate the chocolate-coloured porphyry statue of four stout fellows in armour, complete with long swords and natty pill box hats, on a corner of the famous basilica. The two that have beards are probably the senior ones, Diocletian and Maximian, the clean-shaven chaps the juniors, Galerius and Constantius. The statue is one of the places hordes of tourists like to stop for a selfie. But these four fellows have no place in Venice at all. They were made to be displayed in Constantinople, now Istanbul, part of the public show of finery for the Roman court there. In 1204 the Venetians sacked the city during the Fourth Crusade – even though it was Christian – and spent three days looting, murdering and raping. The statue of the tetrarchs was one trophy they plundered. Another stands close by on the basilica loggia, the 'Horses of Saint Mark', actually four bronze statues of horses originally from a race course. Though the ones you see now are a replica – to meet the magnificent originals you have to go into the first floor museum in the basilica, a wondrous place many visitors miss.

Diocletian, the senior of the pack, came up with the tetrarchy as a way of instilling some stability into the running of the vast territory of the empire, too big, he understood, to be managed by one man alone. Those four figures in Venice are hugging one another like the best of friends. Nothing could be further from the truth.

It's not easy to distil the complexities of Roman politics at the beginning of the fourth century AD into a few paragraphs. By this stage the empire looked more than ever like a criminal enterprise carved up among warring mafia factions than a functioning political state.

In 305 both Diocletian and Maximian abdicated and supposedly retired from the scene. In 306 Constantius died at York after a spell of fighting Picts in northern England and made very sure before he expired that the army would declare his son Constantine his successor. By 308 seven different men, Galerius, Constantine, the supposedly retired Maximian, Maxentius, the son of Maximian, a rising star called Licinius and two also-rans, Maximinus Dia and Domitius Alexander, were in contention with each other for the reins of the empire.

The four stern-faced tetrarchs in that close embrace on a corner of the Piazza San Marco have their hands clutched firmly round the hilts of their finely decorated swords as they watch the teeming masses of tourists pass by snapping their selfies. Soon it would be time to turn them on each other.

HISTORY HAS PAINTED Marcus Aurelius Valerius Maxentius Augustus – Maxentius to his friends and enemies – as one of the bad guys. This is because history, as ever, is written by winners. The victor in this case being Constantine, who turned the empire into a Christian state. As a consequence, his hagiographers made Maxentius a cruel villain, guilty of persecuting Christians like the pagan he was. The fellow was no angel – a saintly nature was not conducive to staying alive in imperial circles at this, or pretty much any other time. But there's little to suggest he actively picked on Christians or anyone else for their religion.

Constantine, on the other hand, had his own wife and son executed, for reasons no one quite understands. He was also an inveterate looter of anywhere with something he fancied, especially pagan temples.

One of the principal differences between the two is that Constantine was a man of the east, much happier there than in the grubby, teeming squalor of Rome. Whereas Maxentius was firmly rooted in what was still – just – the capital of the empire, as a walk along today's Via Appia very clearly demonstrates.

Between the second and third miles of the road, just after the church and catacombs of San Sebastiano as you head away from the city, lie the remains of what's known as the Circus of Maxentius. This was once home to a huge stadium, second only to the Circus Maximus in size. For once it's easy to imagine what the original looked like. The remains of the starting boxes for the chariots are still visible, along with the *spina*, the raised central barrier around which they raced. Ten thousand spectators could have come here to enjoy the spectacle, though in reality it was little used. Perhaps just once, for the funeral games marking the death of Maxentius's beloved young son, Romulus, whose circular mausoleum still stands next to the stadium, close to the ruins of his father's expansive villa. That was meant to be the burial place for Maxentius too, the emperor of Rome. It was not to be.

In the brief years Maxentius was effective monarch of Italy, a title disputed by Constantine among others, the estate on the Via Appia was his grand and very public display of the power and status he'd attained. The Romans loved him at first, often a sign their loyalty would one day wane. While other players in the power game of the time, like Constantine, lived and ruled elsewhere, taking little interest in the city that began the empire, Maxentius painted himself as Roman through and through. He'd seized power in the vacuum created by the lack of interest in Rome among his rivals, promising to save its citizens from the taxation being levied on cities elsewhere. He was also a keen builder, as the monuments on the Via Appia and in the Forum demonstrate, calling himself 'conservator urbis suae', preserver of the city.

It was always a disputed crown – even his own father-in-law, Galerius, one of the tetrarchs, fought against him. But by then the tetrarchy itself was beginning to fall apart, as was much of the empire. Rome had stretched her grasping fists so far in every direction seeking territory, riches and domination, it sometimes seemed there was no one left to fight but one another.

In the spring of 312 Constantine invaded through the Alps. One by one the cities north of Rome either fell or capitulated to his forces. Maxentius, short of money to fund his building programme, and faced with the need to impose unpopular taxes on the city, was no longer the local hero. The pivotal battle took place on October 28th. According to the Christian historians, Constantine, still a pagan himself, had a dream the night before, one that promised him victory if he fought beneath the Christian standard.

Maxentius chose to take a stand on the far side of the Tiber, by a pontoon bridge he'd built for his troops. There's a river crossing still near that point today, the Ponte Milvio, which gave the engagement its name, the Battle of the Milvian Bridge. It's a suburban spot in the north of the city, best known today for the busy flea market. What happened here in 312 AD changed the face of the world more than any single event in Roman history. Constantine, under his Christian banner, was victorious. Maxentius's troops were pushed back onto a makeshift wooden bridge which collapsed under their weight pitching him into the Tiber where he drowned.

Rome fell to the invaders. Christianity was on its way to becoming the sole faith of the empire. And that empire would soon begin to forget the city that created it.

CONSTANTINE LOVED HIS MONUMENTS. His glorious triumphal arch by the Colosseum remains one of the best-preserved and most-photographed sights in all of Rome. Finished two years after his victory at the Milvian Bridge, it's a grandiose piece of propaganda twenty one metres high and twenty six wide, the largest triumphal arch still standing. The inscription and the statuary all serve to tell the tale of Constantine's greatness, and how worthy he is of being counted alongside his famous predecessors such as Hadrian and Marcus Aurelius.

It's also a great testament to his fondness for nicking the work of others and calling it his own. The sculptures which seem to show him at war or carrying out his imperial duties were mostly pinched from earlier monuments, with the face of earlier emperors recut to resemble his own. A little way along the forum you'll find the remains of the vast building known as the Basilica Nova, once the Basilica of Constantine, though more accurately that of Constantine and Maxentius. It was the man he defeated at the Milvian Bridge who began this massive complex and had almost finished it when he died in the chilly waters of the Tiber. Constantine paid for the final touches and turned it into another monument to his greatness, with a colossal statue of himself seated on a throne. You can still see the head and a lone foot – and quite a size they are – in the Capitoline Museums.

For all his enthusiasm to see his victory commemorated in Rome, Constantine didn't much like the place. Over time it came to hate him too. In 326, the same year he had his son Crispus and wife Fausta murdered, he made a rare visit to the city and offended the locals by insulting an annual pagan procession to the Capitol. As the locals swore and grumbled, he vowed never to return. His new capital was on the site of Byzantium, to be renamed Constantinople, what else? The end of a vast military, political and social enterprise sparked by an ingenious piece of road-building six centuries before was in sight.

THE ROMAN EMPIRE had already started to collapse under its own unwieldy weight. Christianity and Constantine simply pulled out the first few bricks. By the end of the fourth century the focus of government had shifted firmly away from Rome. What was left of the centralised power structure which once held the empire's territories together vanished in bickering, vendettas and struggles for control. In 410 the city was sacked by the Gothic troops of Alaric, once a Roman commander himself. Sixty six years later another former foreign Roman officer, the German Oadacer, became king of Italy. A barbarian was on the throne.

Failed states have no need of extensive road networks, commercial arteries that are costly and difficult to maintain. All those careful engineering works, the drainage schemes, the rules about repairs and how they were to be paid for belonged to another era. The connected consular roads of old were abandoned unless they served some local purpose. For the next millennium and more Italy would turn into a patchwork of rival city states employing mercenary *condottieri* to fight wars across a jigsaw of borders more complex than any Appius Claudius Caecus had ever seen in the tribes of the Samnites and the Etruscans in the third century BC.

By the middle of the fifth century the population of Rome had tumbled from a million at its imperial peak to a quarter of that. Little more than a century later that had fallen to around fifty thousand. The great buildings of the Forum crumbled or were pillaged for their masonry and statues. Over time the ground level rose and grass grew on the earth, so richly it was used as pasture for cattle. What was once the focal point of Europe's greatest empire became known as the *campo vacino,* the field of cows.

In the eleventh century around thirty thousand people lived within the city walls. The *caput mundi* was little more than a miserable, unimportant, crumbling shadow of its past and remained that way until a new generation of popes and gentry began to rebuild and repopulate the city during the Renaissance. Rome would not become capital of a reunited Italy again until 1871, more than fifteen hundred years after Maxentius died in the Tiber at the Milvian Bridge.

～

OVER THE CENTURIES, the Queen of Roads lost her crown. Where tombs and temples had something of value, it was stolen. Where there was nothing to pillage, nature was left to overcome the careful engineering and roadwork of old. There's no better or more beautiful place to experience this than a curious testament to the Appia's fall on the Pontine Marshes past Cisterna di Latina on the way to the coast.

Ninfa was adored by the Romans as the site of a temple for river spirits. On the back of traffic along the ancient road – and the money that brought – the place grew into a busy and important town. While the rest of the Via Appia declined, that route from city to sea at Terracina continued and even prospered for a while after the old empire was dead. Ninfa was one of the beneficiaries, rising in medieval times to be able to boast seven churches within its walls and two beyond. They were built in gratitude by Pope Alexander III who was elected pontiff there in 1159, avoiding a Rome racked by riots caused by a rival candidate for the throne.

The location, with its lakes and river and fine buildings, was idyllic but the future, like so many similar communities along the Via Appia, proved bleak. Alexander's election infuriated Frederick Barbarossa, the Holy Roman Emperor, who wanted another man to wear the papal crown. Frederick's troops sacked Ninfa and from that point on the town fell into disrepair. There were no tithes to be collected from travellers on the Via Appia, no churches left to maintain the rule of the clerics. Ninfa never regained her fortunes. For one thing, the growing constant presence of malaria on the marshes that were encroaching on the Pontine area made it an inhospitable place to live.

By the twentieth century the estate was still in the hands of the Caetani, the aristocratic clan that had owned it for many generations, the same Caetani who once ruled the roost from the fortress by the tomb of Caecilia Metella. Along came Gelasio Caetani who decided to bring Ninfa back to life not as a working town but a beautiful garden. Today it's still in family hands and a mecca for knowing horticultural devotees from around the world, attracted by an astonishing and exotic range of flowers, shrubs and trees, all set within the ruins of old Ninfa's churches, houses and castle. A haunting echo of the Via Appia's glorious past.

~

NINFA IS FAR from the only ghost along the Via Appia. On the wall of the wonderful circular crusader's church of San Giovanni al Sepolcro in Brindisi there's a map setting out the route that pilgrims to the Holy Land gradually established over the centuries. A 13th-century traveller's notebook records the journey across the Adriatic to Corfu then on to Crete, Rhodes, Cyprus, Beirut, Acre and finally Jerusalem. The devout, the military and the simply curious thought nothing of traversing the medieval world across great distances along proven paths, provisioned with lodgings, hospitals and church organisations to cater for them.

Over time, the pilgrim journey became known as the Via Francigena and ran from Canterbury and the shrine of Thomas Becket, through France and Switzerland into Italy, then on to Rome and Brindisi. Parts used the old consular roads where they were still passable. But often they were gone, 'rotta', broken in Italian, 'rupta' in Latin, which is why the track of the journey came to be known as a 'route'. Today the Via Francigena is being resurrected with help from the Council of Europe and local bodies, setting out walking, cycling and public transport options to travel from the white cliffs of Dover to Rome then on to the pillars that mark the end of the Via Appia in Brindisi. Another cycle-only route, EuroVelo 5, runs from Canterbury to Brussels and Alsace, on through the Alps into Italy, with a planned section following much of the route of the Via Appia from Benevento into Brindisi.

There's even been talk of trying to resurrect the old road itself for walking all the way from Rome to the south. An ambitious project, perhaps an unrealistic one given the scale of the idea and the obstacles. Italy is so full of history and opportunities to bring the past to the surface. Only a few of those can possibly attract the resources to make them happen. Appius may have built the first section of his road to Capua in five years. But it would take many more than that, and a lot of money, to bring his creation back to life today.

Still, it's a pleasant dream... who knows?

～

THAT'S the thing about the open road. It tempts you. A dead straight line stretching into the distance makes you ask… what if I go somewhere new? Talk to different people? Hear fresh voices, try to understand the ways others see the world? To explore life beyond my own small experience of it? What if, instead of staying put, I embark upon a journey to investigate the unknown?

Roads spark that very human – and very Roman – attribute curiosity. They entice you to venture beyond the near and try to understand the far. When I first began driving my little Abarth up and down the Via Appia, I thought I was looking to unearth a relic, a monument, a fossil lurking beneath the patina of centuries, the grass and the earth of an encroaching countryside, the asphalt and construction of the twenty-first century. It was only later, when I was beyond the tourist trails, staring at the empty wilds of Campania and Basilicata, appreciating the scale of Appius's enterprise, that I realised this was a false and pointless aspiration. It doesn't matter that much of the Via Appia has vanished. What's important is its legacy and the lessons left behind.

We often idealise Rome as the bringer of civilisation to an inarticulate, primordial world, leading it out of darkness into a benign, informed enlightenment. This is simplistic and in many ways downright false. The Romans were in it for themselves, and never ashamed to admit the fact. They were an avaricious, violent race, eager to subdue and colonise in their own interests, never those of anyone else's. Those who stood in their way either died, were assimilated or became slaves. Yet slaves and the colonised learn lessons too, and it's no coincidence that, when the empire finally fell, it was to so-called barbarians often schooled in war by the legions they finally defeated. Rome didn't so much bring civilisation to Europe; it gave other nations the means to find civilisation for themselves.

The invention of fast, reliable arteries that delivered people and goods, armies and commerce rapidly from one strategic location to another – not simply the next place along the way – helped transform a patchwork of inward-looking, primeval tribes into the world we recognise today. It was the beginning of the complex web of relationships that forms the structure of modern life, of conjoined economic, social and political interests. That ease and freedom of movement made for an intermingling of languages and faiths, the sharing of ideas about philosophy and science, government and morality. And yes, it's a prolix, occasionally unbalanced system that can lead to conflict, wars and, as recent events have shown, dreadful pandemics as easily, sometimes, as it offers peace and prosperity. Yet the road is only a highway; the purpose we travel it is always down to us. In a way, the Via Appia proved to be the ancient equivalent of the internet, a disruptive and unstoppable force, for the better mostly, and sometimes, when the darker side of human nature became uppermost, for the worse. A genie let out of the bottle that could never be put back.

Most of all though one thing struck me as I wandered up and down its length, marvelling at the stories of emperors like Augustus and Tiberius, the courage and defiance of Spartacus and his slave brothers, astonished time and time again by the scale and the sophistication of the enterprises undertaken by individuals my old school teachers used to label 'primitives'. The Via Appia remains a reminder that people who have the liberty to move and trade, live and learn, begin families and raise new hopes, regardless of the often artificial borders that confine them, are the ones who take us forward. Not just the famous wearing their imperial togas, hands firmly round the reins of power. But the millions of ordinary people who built those roads and risked their futures and occasionally their lives to follow them.

The Jews who ventured from Jerusalem to set up trade in foreign capitals. The soldiers from Africa who fought and died in distant Scotland. The evangelists who trod its cobbles to Rome knowing they might never see home again and could face a cruel martyrdom. The slaves who lived under the whip and, if they were lucky, became freedmen, rich enough to leave memorials that still stand alongside those of the mighty in Rome today.

The enduring lesson of the Via Appia is one we so easily forget: that we progress through building roads and bridges, not by hiding behind higher and more formidable walls.

Appius Claudius Caecus was fond of telling his fellow Romans more than two thousand three hundred years ago 'quisque faber suae fortunae'. Every man is the architect of his own fortune. What he could never have guessed is that he'd also prove to be the architect of ours.

INFORMATION FOR TRAVELLERS

An extensive album of David's photos taken while researching this book and a live, interactive map of the locations are available at www.davidhewson.com/appian. Internet connections are required for both. The map may be best viewed using the free Google Earth app on phones and tablets. Press 'Present' to start the slide show.

TAKE YOUR TIME

HORACE SAID, 'The Appian Way is less work if you travel slowly.' Two thousand years on, that's still excellent advice. If you think you can do this entire itinerary in a week, you're deluded. The regional park outside Rome could easily consume that alone.

Two weeks is probably the minimum for the whole journey, but be creative and don't think you need to tackle it in a logical, linear fashion. You can book one-way car hire from any of the main airports, picking up a vehicle in Rome, say, and leaving it in Brindisi. That costs a lot more than returning the vehicle to the place you hired it. I picked up my little Abarth at Fiumicino − the car wasn't available at most other outlets − for little more than £13 a day. Then I drove down to Brindisi ticking off some sights along the way, and came back ticking off the rest. I was glad I did because inevitably you miss something in one direction, and it was easy enough to catch up with it on the return.

Planning is pretty much essential unless you want to find yourself panicking as you try to find a room at the end of a busy day. Book ahead − accommodation is sparse on some parts of the journey. Even when it isn't, a simple public holiday can mean hotels are full. Starchy and boring as it sounds, a proper itinerary based on the sights you want to see, allowing reasonable time to get there, with reserved accommodation locally may be a lot less work than trying to make up your trip as you go.

SIGHTS ALONG THE WAY

This is a selective list of some of the principal sights open to visitors along the route of the original Via Appia from Rome to Brindisi. There is, of course, much else besides. For a highly-detailed guide to every mile I recommend the Getty Museum's *The Appian Way, From Its Foundation to the Middle Ages*. This is the most comprehensive book on the Via Appia available in English, an exhaustive listing of just about everything one might wish to see from north to south, with maps, photographs and archaeological and historical detail. Unfortunately, it's only available in a large format hardback edition which is a little awkward for travelling.

Always check online that the places you're aiming to see are actually open since closures for refurbishment are common. Many museums close on Mondays. National museums are usually free the first Sunday of every month.

Porta San Sebastiano. This was originally called the Porta Appia since it was the gate through which the Via Appia passes, as it still does today. The flood of pilgrims to visit the relics of Saint Sebastian led to the name change in the fifteenth century. Today's structure of two circular towers dates back to its original construction in the third century as part of the Aurelian Walls. It houses the Museo della Mura, the Museum of the Wall, with archaeological exhibits, mosaics and, best of all, a wonderful view from the tower. Entry is currently free, closed Mondays and at 2pm in the afternoon.

Parco Regionale dell'Appia Antica. This vast park currently covers more than four and a half thousand hectares which include a long stretch of the Via Appia, the Caffarella park, the spectacular remains of two aqueducts, the Aqua Claudia and the Aqua Felix, and the tomb complex of the Via Latina. This is a very varied and complex area which few people will explore completely in one visit. I strongly advise looking at the guides in English that can be downloaded from the park website and deciding what you want to see in advance.

You will find warnings of something the travellers of two thousand years ago would have recognised too. Back then there were bandits and dodgy characters out on the fringes. It's the same today. At night some outlying areas are notorious as pick-up points for sex workers and the less salubrious side of Rome. A fleeting army of homeless people flit through the shadows, a side of the city many visitors barely witness. This does provide the occasional curious sight: a friend of mine once saw a group of homeless refugees set up a makeshift cricket pitch with a wicket, a ball and a couple of bats, out on the fields which were once part of some rich nobleman's estate.

But don't be put off. This applies only to a few places at the very edge and at night, when no visitor would want to go anyway. The Caffarella valley is popular with joggers, dog walkers, and cyclists, not quite as solitary as it might first seem, and dotted with hidden historical gems. The main focus for tourists, the part of the Via Appia running from the Porta San Sebastiano to the tomb of Caecilia Metella, is adequately served by buses, with cafes and restaurants here and there.

The section up to the Catacombs of San Sebastiano is, however, narrow and congested with traffic. Walking is difficult and cycling not much better. The easiest way to get around is on bus using an unlimited ticket. After San Sebastiano traffic is much lighter and walking a delight to sights such as the Circus of Maxentius and the Tomb of Caecilia Metella and beyond. But do wear a pair of sturdy shoes – the Sampietrini stones of the road were made for carts more than walking.

If you want to fit in a side trip to the tombs of the Via Latina, a short stretch of historic road that's probably a closer approximation to the Via Appia of old, it's a very quick bus ride on the 660 from the stop opposite the friendly little cafe on the corner before the free and very quiet Capo di Bove information point after Caecilia Metella. Access is free but you will only get to see inside the tombs, with their lovely frescoes, if you book on an open weekend through the Coop Culture website.

The Alban Hills. Castel Gandolfo is the primary tourist attraction for the Pope's summer palace. But there are Roman remains throughout the area, around the lakes of Nemi and Albano. The village of Nemi is a lovely stop, with a few bed and breakfast places and wonderful views. The museum dedicated to Caligula's ships is a hilly walk from the village and well worth it.

Ninfa. Frequently lauded as one of the most beautiful gardens in the world, Ninfa sits among the ruins of an old way station along the Via Appia. Only open April to November. Advance booking required.

Terracina. A bustling seaside town with a historic centre where the original Via Appia still runs through what was once the forum. The temple of Jupiter Anxur overlooking the town is a must.

Sperlonga. Principally a small beach resort, Sperlonga is also home to a museum housing the remains of the villa of Tiberius and the grotto in which he nearly lost his life. The recreated statues from the grotto in the museum are fascinating if probably a little imaginative in their execution.

Gaeta and Formia. Busy coastal towns a few miles apart on an attractive bay, perfect for a seaside break on the itinerary. Gaeta is the more spectacular, dominated by the peak of Monte Orlando with the mausoleum of wily old Plancus. Formia, badly damaged during the Second World War, is the more peaceful, with a good local museum and the site of Cicero's 'mausoleum' and his former villa. It's easy to flit between the two on a local bus.

Minturno. An important waypoint on the Via Appia. The old road still runs through the archaeological site which has an amphitheatre, copious ruins and an interesting museum.

Santa Maria Capua Vetere (Capua). Once one of the most important cities in Roman Italy, now a sleepy small town with a different name. The amphitheatre is second in size to the Colosseum, part of an extensive archaeological complex that also includes an excellent restaurant. The mithraeum is well worth seeing – book a slot through the ticket office in the amphitheatre.

Caserta. Just along the road from old Capua and strictly speaking nothing to do with the Via Appia – it only came into being around the eighth century AD. The Royal Palace for the Bourbon Kings is an Italian Versailles, an elegant complex often used in movie sets.

Benevento. Set in an attractive position by the Calore river, Benevento is the old capital of the Samnites, now a pleasant university city best known in Italy for the legend of its local witches. The museum has an excellent display of Roman and Samnite exhibits. The Arch of Trajan commemorates the victories of the emperor and marks the point at which he established a branch of the Via Appia which went to Brundisium by the coast through modern Bari. The Roman amphitheatre is well worth a visit, as is the picturesque original bridge nearby.

Aeclanum. Once an important town for the Hirpini tribe before they were conquered by the Romans, this is now a small archaeological site in Passo di Mirabella.

Venosa. An important way station on the Via Appia, now a genial, remote town in southern Basilicata. Venusia was the birthplace of the poet Horace, Orazio in Italian, who's commemorated throughout the town. There's an extensive archaeological site next to later church ruins. Jewish catacombs – which can only be visited by appointment – indicate the presence of a large Jewish community between the fourth and sixth centuries AD. There's a small display about Venosa's Jewish heritage in the interesting museum inside the town's imposing Aragonese castle.

Gravina in Puglia. Twenty miles from Venosa on the road south. The setting on the edge of a ravine is spectacular, as are the sights, which are mostly post-Roman, the best-known being the church of San Michele dei Grotti which is carved out of the tuff rock face.

Matera. The biggest tourist draw of the region, and one destined to become even more popular after its starring role in the Bond movie *No Time To Die*. The highly visual ravine location and cave houses have made Matera popular with film makers for decades. The Via Appia ran past the town and there are no relevant sights there connected to it. But it could make a convenient if touristy place to stay.

Taranto. Polluted, grubby and chaotic, modern Taranto bears little resemblance to the beautiful Greek and Roman city of old. The city museum has a wonderful collection of exhibits going back to its days as a Spartan stronghold. The Old Town, the original island guarding the channels from the inner lagoon to the sea, is being tidied up and has several interesting underground sites and a lively, bohemian nightlife. Easily visited by train from Brindisi – the journey is only an hour or so.

Brindisi. The last stop on the Via Appia. A large but agreeable port city with a fascinating old quarter made for wandering. Small ferries run around the picturesque harbour to outlying districts. The city museum is one of the best along the length of the Via Appia. There are several interesting churches, including the circular San Giovanni al Sepolcro established by the Templars on their return from Jerusalem.

GETTING AROUND BY CAR

The five most important pieces of advice I'd give to anyone driving this route:

1. Hire the smallest car you can manage. You'll be using roads that are narrow and discovering the Italian attitude towards parking, one which does not share the same space time continuum – especially the space part – as the rest of us. Tempting as that Maserati Ghibli might appear at Fiumicino, it's not going to be a great idea.

2. View your trip down the Via Appia as a succession of destinations, not an attempt to follow every mile of the original road. This isn't practical and attempting to do so will only waste valuable time for no real reward.

3. With the previous point in mind... plan. Pick the places you want to go, key them into your satnav then make sure it's set to take you there the fastest way not the shortest (which won't be fast at all). You won't follow the original road exactly but it'll be close enough and you'll save yourself the pain of finding yourself down a dirt track staring at a herd of goats. Always treat the satnav's recommendations with care. They will usually be spot on for the main routes but out in the wilds of Basilicata may be rather less reliable.

4. Check the parking. Many hotels and bed and breakfasts will blithely say 'free parking outside'. This may just mean if you

can find a space you can use it. And if there isn't one you'll spend ages circling somewhere you don't know trying to find a place to park.

5. Don't take your car into Rome. You don't need it and you won't enjoy it. Brindisi is fine for driving, provided you know where you're going to park (see the hotel recommendations below). Taranto is a lot more difficult – check ahead on Google Maps Street View so you have an idea where you're headed. Get lost in the Old Town and you'll be in a circular system that seems endless.

Driving in Italy is nothing like as frightening as some people seem to think. Stick to the speed limits – there are lots of cameras around and any fines will go on your credit card. Make sure you're properly insured. Stay in the slow lane and enjoy the scenery.

PUBLIC TRANSPORT

A fair bit of the Via Appia can be reached without a car provided you have the time and are willing to plan. In Rome, public transport is the only sane option. The regional park area of the Appia Antica beyond the Porta San Sebastiano is accessible by local buses which can be used on a cheap all-in ticket available from machines at stations and tobacconists. There's also a regular commuter rail line from Termini, Rome's central station, and Ciampino airport out into the Alban Hills, stopping at Castel Gandolfo and terminating at Albano Laziale. You'd then need to take a taxi to Ariccia and Nemi.

Regular trains run from Rome and Naples to the station Monte S. Biagio-Terracina Mare which is a cheap fifteen minute bus ride from Terracina town. Local buses also take you along the coast to Sperlonga and Gaeta. At Formia you can pick up the train again or try other buses. From Minturno-Scauri station a couple of stops will take you to Santa Maria Capua Vetere (Capua) in ninety minutes if you manage to get the direct train to Caserta, or two hours if you have to change in Aversa. Return to Caserta and there's a one-hour direct service to Benevento.

At this point things get sticky. There is a circuitous and infrequent bus service via Foggia to Maschito, a five-mile cab ride from Venosa. Or you could try to take a three-hour train and bus journey to Melfi via Foggia. But this is a lot of awkward travelling on sporadic services. Unless you have the time and enjoy prolix bus journeys I'd be tempted to skip Basilicata and take the fastest train route to Brindisi, stay there and visit Taranto for the day – an hour away by regular train. The high speed Frecciargento express will take you from Brindisi back to Rome in five hours.

Often it's cheaper to book ahead with a discount on the Trenitalia website. But there are various rail passes available too, though check out any restrictions they have on the use of high speed services such as the Frecciargento.

ACCOMMODATION

This isn't a tour guide. There are plenty of sources of information around for that. Long experience has taught me it's often unwise to recommend hotels and restaurants in Italy since they often change with the wind. I will, however, mention four places I stayed on my journeys which stood out both for service but also because they were extremely convenient for the sights. In Brindisi, the historic Grande Albergo Internazionale is in a perfect location by the harbour, very close to the end of the Via Appia. It's a posh place that's a little care-worn but you can't beat the position. You can just turn up in your car, leave it outside and, for a fee, they will park it overnight.

The Villa Irlanda between Gaeta and Formia is similarly convenient, with plenty of free parking and a variety of rooms set in grounds that cover what was once the estate of Augustus's stepfather. While the address is given as Gaeta it's actually closer to Formia with the beach and its restaurants just a pleasant stroll away. In Santa Maria Capua Vetere I stayed right by the amphitheatre in the two-apartment house Casa Vacanze Antica Capua perfectly located and with free parking outside.

In Rome I used the Inn at the Roman Forum in Monti, a short walk from bus stops that will take you quickly to the main destinations of the Via Appia outside the city. The place is very central for all the sights in Rome and comes with its own two-thousand-year-old crypto-porticus. Don't even think of trying to take a car there.

Elsewhere I suggest you scour the usual hotel sites, check out the reviews and the parking if you need it, and cross your fingers. Beyond the main sites places such as Nemi are more likely to offer bed and breakfast in rooms than hotels, with little in the way of services, or fellow tourists for that matter. After a while you'll find it hard to believe you're in the same country as those crowds packed into the Roman Forum, the Piazza San Marco and milling around outside the Uffizi.

Buon viaggio.

ABOUT THE AUTHOR

David Hewson is the author of more than thirty novels, many set in Italy including the acclaimed ten-book Nic Costa crime series. Before becoming an author he was a journalist on the London *Times* and *Sunday Times*.

facebook.com/davidhewsonauthor
twitter.com/david_hewson
instagram.com/david.hewson
youtube.com/DavidHewsonwrites